AUTO FAMOSO DE LA DESCENSIÓN DE NUESTRA SEÑORA EN LA SANTA YGLESIA DE TOLEDO, QUANDO TRUJO LA CASULLA AL GLORIOSSÍSSIMO SAN ILEFONSO SU SANTO ARÇOBISPO Y PATRÓN NUESTRO

(BN Madrid, Ms. Res. 80)

Edited by

Joseph T. Snow

University of Georgia

UNIVERSITY OF EXETER

1983

ISSN 0305 8700

ISBN 0 85989 132 1

Printed by

Short Run Press Ltd, Exeter

April 1983

EXETER HISPANIC TEXTS

General Editors

Keith Whinnom (General and Medieval)

J. M. Alberich (Modern and Hispanoamerican)

W. F. Hunter (Golden Age)

XXX

LA DESCENSIÓN

DE NUESTRA SEÑORA

PREFACE

In an appendix to J. M. Aguirre's *José de Valdivielso y la poesía religiosa tradicional* (Toledo, 1965), mention is made of a manuscript copy of Valdivielso's *Auto famoso de la Descensión* at the Biblioteca Nacional in Madrid. A note (p. 214) states that this *auto* had been edited by Léo Rouanet in 1899. While the title of Rouanet's article, "Un auto inédit de Valdivielso," would suggest that perhaps an edition was involved, such was not the case.[1] The same claim was later made by another of Valdivielso's editors, J. Fleckniakosca.[2]

An edition was prepared for inclusion in the two-volume edition of Valdivielso's *Teatro completo*. To my knowledge, only the first of the planned set is circulating and it contains only works previously printed elsewhere.[3] The present edition is, then, the first of Bib. Nac. MS Res. 80 which is complete. The copy, an autograph dated 1643, was prepared by a friend and fellow playwright of Joseph de Valdivielso, Francisco de Roxas. A later copy also exists in the collection of the Biblioteca Nacional. It is less reliable generally but served well in one or two important ways in the preparation of this edition, carried out in the summers of 1978 and 1982 (and in the interim, from xerographic copies).

I suspect that this *comedia religiosa*—the term is perhaps better applied to this play than is *auto*—which juxtaposes pious in-

dividuals--notably San Ildefonso and the Virgin--with an appealing
gallery of secular comic figures, will have broad appeal to a variety
of scholars. Certainly for the historian of literature with an
interest in the morphology of saints' lives, this play will fill
in another chapter in the continuing Ildefonso story, earlier taken up by Rodrigo, *el Cerratense*, Berceo, Alfonso X, Juan Gil de
Zamora, the Beneficiado de Ûbeda, Martínez de Toledo,[4] López de
Ûbeda and others, and continued not only by Valdivielso but also
by Lope, Góngora, Jáuregui,Ledesma, Espinel, Calderón, and dozens
more.

For the student of Valdivielso's dramatic and poetic craft, the
Descensión will modify and refine what is already known, but especially in the introduction of a lighter mood and the creation of
comic characters. Then, too, for those interested in production
of Golden Age theatre, the *Descensión* would present few problems
in translation to the modern stage. In fact, it ought to prove
as satisfying to today's audiences as to the only one we know for
certain that it had in its own time, in 1616, when it was per-
formed in the presence of King Philip III.

In preparing the introductory sections I have tried to limit
my commentaries to just those affairs of the opening years of the
seventeenth century which affect the moment, the motives, and the
mounting of the open air production of Valdivielso's *Descensión*.
Each of the sections could easily be expanded. Still, as they now
stand, they provide the basic information for the full apprecia-
tion of the play, and of the not inconsequential role it played
in the events in and around Toledo in 1616.

One further point, however, needs to be addressed before pro-
ceeding. Valdivielso, when he sent his *Doze autos sacramentales
y dos comedias divinas* to the printer (1622), did not include the
Descensión. Why not? No mention of any plans to print it is made
in Valdivielso's other writings and, since he lived to 1638, we
may conclude that he had good reasons not to see it into printed
form. I do not believe that Valdivielso judged it unworthy, al-

though this is conjecture on my part. The play is simply too
good for that to seem likely. Since the play was commissioned
for a special occasion, it may have been hurried in the writing:
if so, the author may have held hopes (unrealized) of polishing
it later. Or, possibly, as an occasional piece there may have
been reason to think that a general audience would not appreciate
it as did his public in Toledo where Ildefonso is revered as one
of the city's *santos patrones*. A final possibility will emerge
from the introduction to follow: the play might be a reminder to
Lope, who was a friend of Valdivielso's, of how he was excluded
from the *justas poéticas* of 1616 in Toledo (the same occasion
which prompted the *Descensión*) and how his arch-rival, Góngora,
carried off the prize.

The copy from which Roxas made his is now, apparently, lost.
Doubtless, Roxas knew the play, perhaps had even seen it per-
formed. He made his copy--from Valdivielso's own?--only five
years after the death of his friend, but we do not know what his
motives were. How accurate it is we can only speculate upon. We
may trust a little in the friendship, I think, and to his valu-
ation of a colleague's art, to strengthen our hope that the text,
as here presented, will be a fair representation of what Joseph
de Valdivielso actually wrote. In presenting it, I should like
to echo Valdivielso's own words from his prefatory remarks to the
Doze autos sacramentales, and apply them to this other work from
his pen, the *Descensión*: "No pienso que desmerecerán estos Actos
impressos el buen pasage que gozaron representados."[5]

Acknowledgments of my debts to others are in order. I thank
my colleague, John C. Dowling, for taking the time to have both
of the manuscripts copied for my use at home when I know he had
other matters pressing. For special considerations and much help
in locating references, I owe the staff of the Sección de Raros
at the Biblioteca Nacional a large debt of gratitude. To the
editors of this series, special thanks for patience with delays
(all mine) and for unusually helpful advice in the editing of the

text. Finally, I have worked on this project in spare moments in Georgia, Wisconsin, London, and Madrid: I especially need to thank the staff of Wisconsin's Institute for Research in the Humanities for the time and space they provided me during 1978-1979 and in the summers of 1981 and 1982, where time and again I was able to pick up the threads of my progress.

NOTES

1. See *Homenaje a Menéndez y Pelayo,* I (Madrid, 1899), 57-62.

2. See his edition of *El hospital de los locos* and *La serrana de Plasencia* (Salamanca: Anaya, 1971), 29-30.

3. *Teatro completo,* I, edited by Ricardo Arias and Robert Piluso (Madrid: Isla, 1976).

4. The *Vida* of Ildefonso in Castilian, long attributed to Martínez de Toledo, is probably the work of someone else, according to Ralph P. DeGorog, "La atribución de las *Vidas de San Ildefonso y San Isidoro* al Arcipreste de Talavera," *Bol. de la Real Academia Española,* 58 (1978), 169-193.

5. From the "Al Lector" section (no pagination) of Valdivielso's *Doze autos sacramentales y dos comedias divinas* (Toledo: Juan Ruiz, 1622).

INTRODUCTION

> Y aquí, ceñida de laurel y oliva,
> sacras historias Valdivieso escriba.
>
> Lope de Vega
> Canto xix, *Jerusalén conquistada*

1. VALDIVIELSO, SANDOVAL Y ROJAS, PHILIP III, AND SAN ILDEFONSO

Although born in Aranda del Duero (1546), and educated in Alcalá
and Salamanca, the Cardenal Archbishop of Toledo, Bernardo Sandoval
y Rojas revered his adoptive city, especially its Cathedral--the
Primate Church of all Spain[1]--and the city's two patron saints:
Leocadia and Ildefonso. Sandoval y Rojas was surely, because of
his position, one of the most influential men of his day. Even before his nomination to the See of Toledo in 1599, he was a favorite
of Philip III and came to hold the offices of Counselor to the
King, Lord High Chancellor of Castile, and Inquisitor General in
Philip's government. From sometime around 1604 until his death in
December of 1618, the Archbishop was served loyally by the same
capellán--also a versatile man of letters--Joseph de Valdivielso
(1560?-1638).[2]

The three men--king, counselor, and chaplain--were to be guest
of honor, patron, and playwright at the production of the *Auto de
la Descensión* in late October of 1616. This occasion was, really,
one of the final acts in the series of religious ceremonies over
a half-century in Toledo that involve in one way or another the

figure of San Ildefonso. Involved also were royalty, high-level
civil and ecclesiastic dignitaries, and men of letters.

An early event was the return from France to Toledo, on November 18, 1565, into the hands of Philip II, of the bodily remains
of San Eugenio III, an uncle and predecessor of Ildefonso's in
the See of Toledo in the mid-seventh century. Shortly thereafter,
also during the reign of Philip II, came the return of the bodily
remains of Leocadia (1587), sent from Flanders by way of Italy.
The *relatorio* of the festivities held in Toledo tells us that
dramatic presentations were staged at this time, as well as the
almost obligatory poetry competition. The latter produced many
poems recalling the role Leocadia played in the Toledan miracles
of San Ildefonso.[3] Supervising the events celebrating Leocadia's
restoration to her native soil was Sandoval y Rojas' predecessor,
Gaspar Quiroga. It was Quiroga who conceived the idea of build-
ing within the Cathedral a special chapel to honor the Virgen
del Sagrario, a chapel he did not live to see realized.

Sandoval y Rojas, too, had ambitious ideas for restoring parts
of the Cathedral: the sacristy, the vestuary, and the *ochavo* all
were improved under his direction, as were the altar and chapel
consecrated to the descent of Mary in the time of Ildefonso.
Still, what remained as the centerpiece in his renewal of the
Cathedral at Toledo was his making a reality of Quiroga's plans
for the Sagrario chapel, a project finished in 1616.[4]

For the collocation of the image in its new resting place, the
archbishop spared little effort. The ambitious round of activi-
ties for the two week period from October 20 to November 3 included the *certamen poético*, several balls, special sermons,
triumphal arches and fireworks, parades and bullfights, music,
masques, and theatrical entertainments.[5] For at least part of
that time, November 26 and after, the events could be termed
'royal' since the archbishop had provided for the presence of
Philip III and a large court retinue. In fact, Philip often
dignified ceremonies in Toledo sponsored by his Counselor.

However, apart from the special political relationship that may have prompted Philip's attendance in Toledo in October of 1616, it seems at least as likely that, as a religious man, he might have taken a personal interest in them, since they would be featuring Ildefonso, a saint in whom Philip had a special trust.[6] Knowing of this special devotion, the archbishop may have encouraged his chaplain, Valdivielso, to make the two plays he was writing particularly pleasing to Philip. Apparently Valdivielso succeeded.

Here is a brief excerpt from the long description of the events as recorded by Pedro de Herrera. It follows a section which narrates the reception of the image of the Virgen del Sagrario, borne on a richly-adorned *carro*, inside the Cathedral.

> Quedó el carro en medio de la Capilla, con generales
> muestras de alegría universal, dándose parabienes unos
> a otros, y todos al Cardenal. Tornaron acompañando a
> su Magestad y Altezas hasta la entrada (por el claustro)
> al passadizo de la Casa Arçobispal, donde los tuvo
> por huéspedes, haziendo el gasto a todas las personas
> y oficios de ambas casas reales con no menor ánimo y
> opulencia, estimando este día por el más feliz de
> quantos ha tenido, si bien en algunos recibió seme-
> jantes favores de los reyes (...) Por la tarde, en-
> tre las casas del Cardenal y del Ayuntamiento, la
> compañía de Cebrián representó dos autos del Maestro
> Joseph de Valdivielso. Uno de la Descensión de Nues-
> tra Señora a dar la casulla a San Ilefonso = otro,
> de la milagrosa aparición de la Imagen Santa del
> Sagrario, después de haber estado escondida como se
> ha dicho. Viéronlos su Magestad y Altezas de las
> primeras rejas del Cardenal; *fueron de mucho gusto*
> por el argumento tan destos días, y por los bailes
> y sainetes con que aquella compañía regozija sus
> actos cómicos . . . (fol. 87v-88v, emphasis mine).[7]

The two plays were probably presented in this order since the action in the *Descensión* takes place during Ildefonso's lifetime (607-667) and the action of the *Milagrosa Aparición* has as its backdrop the period of Alfonso VI and the reconquest of Toledo (1085). Public interest in the plays may well have been intensified for those who realized that the event the plays were written to commemorate was, if fact, a third chapter in the history of the holy effigy of the Virgen del Sagrario. The story of these three chapters is succinctly told by Pedro de Herrera:

> A esta sacrosancta imagen, abraçada de la Virgen, vene-
> rada por tal de Reyes propios y estraños, de toda España
> y universalmente de las naciones religiosas que el mun-
> do tiene; en cuya presencia, delante el altar mayor
> (primer assiento suyo) viniendo a los maitines llegava
> a orar el santo arçobispo Ilefonso, quando baxó la
> misma soberana Señora a honrarle con la celestial ca-
> sulla, dexando santificado y glorioso el Catedral,
> metropolitano, y primado templo de Toledo. A tan
> preciosa imagen y reliquia santa (que escondida por
> la impiedad Mahometana, manifestaron espíritus an-
> gélicos y celestiales luzes, hallándola en menos
> decente colocación, que según la quietud [ya de
> España] debiera dársele), fabricó el Cardenal Capi-
> lla, tabernáculo no igual a la grandeza desta di-
> vina prenda, ni al ánimo de quien se la ofrecía
> mas el primero en gasto, primor de architectura,
> perpetuidad y pulimiento de materiales.[8]

Valdivielso's second play--which corresponds to the second moment, or 'chapter' in this summary--the *Milagrosa Aparición*-- is now lost. The tale follows the destiny of the image embraced by Mary, saved from certain destruction at the hands of the invading Mohammedans in the eighth century and only restored from its hiding place--a pit or well in the Cathedral--by Alfonso VI, his queen, Costanza, and the then archbishop, Bernardo (the coincidence of the name was not lost on Sandoval y Rojas) when the Cathedral was re-consecrated to Christian practice over three centuries later. These events, as well as those recounted by Valdivielso in the *Descensión,* are also set out in great detail in the playwright's epic poem, *Sagrario de Toledo,* composed earlier but published in the same year 1616, in Toledo, by Luis Sánchez.

We are left to imagine the pleasure Sandoval y Rojas took in viewing the lost play, in which an earlier archbishop, bearing his name, figured prominently, and to speculate upon the unrecorded parallels noted between the eleventh and the seventeenth century restorations involving the Virgen del Sagrario. Although unrecorded in the *relatorios,* the parallels were stressed heavily in Valdivielso's *Sagrario.* Indeed, this day surely must have been for the archbishop "el más feliz de quantos ha tenido," as Herrera believed and wrote. This storybook union, on the grounds of the Cathedral, of three of its archbishops, two (Ildefonso, Bernardo) in spirit and in dramatic re-creation, one (Sandoval y Rojas) in person, was a historic event with transcendental meaning for the aging archbishop, even now just two years from his deathbed.

At any rate, although commissioned to produce the two plays for the October festivities, Valdivielso had been long at work on the materials from which they would be fashioned. In 1612, Valdivielso says as much in the dedication to Sandoval y Rojas of the first edition of his *Romancero espiritual.* The work-in-progress had been commissioned by the archbishop to illustrate the glorious role of Toledo in the religious life of Spain and to reaffirm its status (under attack from Seville and Santiago) as Primate Church of all Spain. This is the *Sagrario de Toledo,* mentioned above, which appeared late in 1616, also dedicated to Sandoval y Rojas.

This long work contains 2,918 octavas distributed over twenty-five books. Unlike the earlier *Vida ... de San José* (1604, etc.), which went through many editions, the *Sagrario* was printed only one

other time (Barcelona, 1618) before sinking from sight. It has,
then, never attracted the scholarly attention it deserves. I can
not remedy this lack here, except to point out how much use Valdivielso made of the earlier poem in the writing of his play (see
my notes to the edition, *passim*). It is known that Valdivielso,
and others, re-used earlier verse in later works, but this is
the first time such a relationship has been established between
the little-studied *Sagrario de Toledo* and the play so pleasing
to Philip III.

The *Sagrario*, let it be said now, is a ponderous work, overly
bombastic in parts, puffed out with digressions and overblown
discourse, all in an effort to glorify Toledo, Ildefonso, the
special favor received at the hands of Mary, and the effigy she
left to the city. It was, then, a perfectly reasonable cause
for a work on an epic scale. The repetitious style and the
cadence of seemingly endless octavas produce a tedium that did
not appeal to contemporary audiences.

Having said that, I should also say that perhaps the most sal-
vageable sections are those written for the dialogues in the
work, especially those between Ildefonso and Mary. These are,
interestingly, the ones from which Valdivielso borrowed heavily
in the crafting of the *Descensión*. They are condensed, amplified,
and recontextualized to suit the dramatic action they now accom-
pany. Good taste is employed in the selection. It would have
been tempting to include much more of the *Sagrario* in the text
of the *Descensión*, but Valdivielso holds back. Not only did
he please the king and, presumably, his patron and archbishop,
but I believe he managed--on the level of literary achievement--
to please even himself.

2. ILDEFONSO AND VALDIVIELSO'S AUTO

Informative accounts of the historical and hagiographical Ildefonso are relatively accessible.[9] I will limit, therefore, this
discussion to those portions of the Ildefonso story relevant to

Valdivielso's *Descensión*. It is understood that what follows traces developments in the hagiographic traditions, as little historical data are available that would, in any case, have much bearing on a play written almost seven centuries later.

Unlike Mary the Egyptian and other spectacular sinners, whose exploits made for exciting narratives and strongly didactic closures, Ildefonso was the most nominal of sinners. It is as if he were born to sainthood. His future devotion to the Virgin Mary is signaled in his being delivered to his mother past her age of childbearing, his mother's dedicating his life to Mary, and his eager memorization of the *Ave María* before the age of two. Ildefonso was attentive, studious, and devout. He chose a monastic career against his father's wishes, persisted, and rose to become his Order's abbot, first, and then by acclamation archbishop of Toledo--succeeding his uncle, Eugenio III. There were no dramatic moments of sin of which he might repent in this ideal, model existence, no violent shifts in life style to mark his renewed devotions to Mary, no depths of evil from which he needed to be, at the eleventh hour, snatched by his heavenly protectress.

The central love of his life was always Mary. He composed hymns in her honor and wrote one of the most famed Marian treatises of the Middle Ages, the elegant, eloquent *De perpetua virginitate beatae Mariae*.[10] And such a life could not end unrewarded. His constancy to the Virgin, and its literary and spiritual manifestations are said to be "el hito inicial de toda la literatura mariana en España."[11] Ildefonso's *De virginitate*--the central jewel in his Marian crown--was inspired by a similar work by St. Jerome, in which a heresy attacking Mary's purity was sullying the Christian landscape.[12] In Ildefonso's time, the heresy--if there was one--originates in Gaul and spreads to Spain where the faithful take refuge in the preachments of their most eloquent defender, Ildefonso of Toledo. In his sermons, and in his writings, Ildefonso succeeds in snuffing out the influence of the villainous attacks on Mary, and routing the villains themselves (who, in surviving manuscript illustration from the eleventh century, are depicted as ugly, snarling wretches).[13] Ildefonso--in one literary metamorphosis--actually is portrayed as Mary's paladin, sallying forth to do battle, armed with the steely resources of his arsenal of *colores rhetorici*, fighting the good fight, triumphant under Mary's banner.[14]

Rewards for such valiant bravery are equally grand. While celebrating one December 9   a mass for the feast day of Toledo's patron and martyr, Leocadia, whose mortal remains lay undiscovered somewhere nearby, Ildefonso is interrupted by a great portent. A massive stone levitates miraculously and, from her tomb, radiant and fragrant, veiled but beautiful, emerges the figure of Leocadia herself. Her message is for Ildefonso: *Per te, Ildefonse, vivit domina mea*. Her lady's honor lives on, intact, unsullied; thanks go to Ildefonso. Ildefonso, not quite struck entirely motionless, recovers enough sense to cut from Leocadia's veil, using a knife proffered him by his admiring king, a small segment to mark the miracle.[15]

This miracle heralds another, greater one. On December 18, while en route to the Cathedral to celebrate a midnight mass, or matins in other tellings, accompanied by many of the faithful, the procession is confronted by a blinding brilliance emanating from within. Only Ildefonso dares enter. Seated in the archbishop's *cátedra*, a copy of the *De virginitate* in her hand, is the Virgin, who comes now personally to thank her servant for his valor. She and the host of angels bestow on Ildefonso a seamless garment sent from on high, a scene often depicted by artists in many media.[16] The garment is often a "casulla" but is other times called an "alba."[17]

During this visit, two things mentioned in the *Descensión* occur: 1) Mary leaves a footprint in the stone floor as a sign that her descent was in person (not a vision)[18] and 2) Mary, as she prepares to return to Heaven, embraces an image of herself. The image, we are told, takes on from that time the features of the

Virgin herself. The image--for these reasons--always was able to command special reverence as the events of 1085-1086 and of 1616 demonstrate.

To these miraculous doings, another element in the traditional Ildefonso narration must be added to help explain the presence of the poor in the *Descensión*. A custom Ildefonso is credited with establishing is the daily feeding of thirty indigents, although this may have been a traditional form of an *imitatio Christi* that attaches itself to the life of the saint. Be that as it may, it does portray an Ildefonso who is not removed from the cares of the world around him: on the contrary, he is very much involved in it.

These, then, are a few details from the traditional account of the life of San Ildefonso which are the matrices of the characterization and plot of Valdivielso's *Descensión de la Virgen*. Those familiar with Berceo's account in the *Milagros de Nuestra Señora*, or with Alfonso X's Cantiga 2 or with a number of other tellings, will also be aware that Valdivielso, in ending his account at the point of maximum glory for Ildefonso, has excised a well-known feature of the story: the punishment by death of Ildefonso's vainglorious successor who--unheeding of prohibitions to the contrary-- dons the celestial garment and seats himself in the *cátedra*, consecrated by the Virgin and forbidden to all but Ildefonso's use. This sombre dénouement, and its didactic message, is sacrificed in the play Valdivielso has written. The seventeenth-century dramatist ends with a vision of apotheosis, entirely in keeping with the dramatic progress of his protagonist throughout. The concluding stanzas make this clear in the parallel between Moses and Ildefonso: each is seen descending from a mountain to face an anxious multitude. Valdivielso wrote the play for a happy occasion, for the entertainment of the king, his patron, and the faithful of Toledo *inter alios*. The festive and yet sacred nature of the occasion justifies his special use of the traditional material.

THE 'AUTO DE LA DESCENSION'. The auto of the descent of the Virgin is a charming work of mixed high, middle, and low styles, full

of fun, witty dialogue, and rich spectacle (what else might one
call the appearance of the Virgin surrounded by "mil ánjeles"?).
We do not know that the play was presented without interruption,
for Herrera (page XI) spoke of *bailes* and *sainetes*: these may
have preceded the first play, filled in before the second one,
and concluded when this one ended. Stage directions tell us something about exits and entrances, asides and offstage music, and
there are useful bits on dress and hand-carried props. There are
no references to *carros* or other machinery of the early stage.
Scenic devices may have been fairly minimal since the Cathedral
and the Town Hall--and the plaza joining them, where the play actually took place--offer the original backdrop to the action of
the plays. Though only two angels and a handful of street people
are assigned speaking roles, it seems likely that others were present, milling about, to fill out the roles of the street urchins
(scenes ii and iii) and the illusion of the "mil ánjeles" (xiv).

The tone and style of the play are not nearly as serious as
the summary of the Ildefonso story above would suggest. Ildefonso
himself, of course, is in character, as are the king, Leocadia,
and the Virgin in the principal spectacle scenes. However, more
numerous are the scenes of the milling populace of Toledo at the
fringes of the main action. There are two main groups of secon-
dary characters. The first is the group of street boys seen in
the first few scenes; the second is the group of street beggars
who receive their charity at Ildefonso's door. The common figure
is Moscón, who is captain of the first gang but also is in service
to Ildefonso and must deal with the second gang.

The urchins serve as a roving band of Marian enthusiasts, in-
tent on ferreting out heretics who may still be in Toledo: this
is their link to the main action, for it is they who come upon
the disguised arch-heretics, Braulio and Florindo. Joining them
is a *vieja* who plays a special role in the end of the play, long
after the urchins' roles are played out. In the middle ground
between these two sets of minor characters are the group of sol-

diers who stand watch at the Cathedral on the day when the king is to attend the services for Leocadia.

The last group consists of the heretics, two who travel together and one--their leader--who is in flight from the reactions to his villainy. This latter, Pelagio, remains unrepentant to the end and becomes the didactic focus of this tale (as Siagrio, the vainglorious successor to Ildefonso, was in Berceo's telling). The former are won back to belief, and are permitted to throw off their disguises.

In a relatively brief space of time, Valdivielso juxtaposes this mix of characters and plot actions, but manages to keep them all somehow pointed to the final moment of Ildefonso's apotheosis. Eloquence runs back-to-back with street cant; the earthly contrasts with the divine; the pace shifts from the frenetic to the serene.

As the play opens, the heretics have already been routed. Their forces are in total disarray. But the exposition of all this is handed over to Moscón and the roving street band, the (disguised) heretics, and the militant *vieja*, while Valdivielso prepares for Ildefonso's delayed entrance onto the scene. When this happens, we are listening to the future saint imploring (anachronistically) Mary's aid in the task of ridding Spain of her enemies, a task already largely accomplished. As Ildefonso prepares for the celebration of Leocadia's feast day, the heretics plan to attend, totally unprepared for the miracle which is to so greatly convince them of their wicked ways. Thus through effective use of timing, juxtaposition, and contrast, Valdivielso builds suspense, even while simultaneously presenting vividly original character creations within a traditional story frame.

The Leocadia scene shows Ildefonso at his most effective. It is balanced well by the catalogue of Heavenly personages who sing Ildefonso's praises (496-588) and the return compliment when Ildefonso, in a semi-ecstatic trance, offers up an instant paean to Leocadia's veil (637-660). Later scenes are planned to set off Ildefonso's earthly demeanor, when he displays generosity and love

for the poor, even though the public is aware that most of them
are fakes: the lame can walk, the blind can see, etc. In these
scenes, Moscón emerges as one of the most delightful characters
in the *Descensión*. He is a blend, one part *embustero*, one part
pícaro, and one part *gracioso*. After parading his false bravado
through most of the play, piercing others with his verbal barbs
and indulging in personal aggrandizement at others' expense, the
portents of the Virgin's descent turn him into the coward we suspect him to be. His confession is a splendid self-parody and
the reader relishes it, remembering the earlier Moscón. That
Valdivielso has him disappear from the play at this point is a
master stroke of characterization: it strengthens one of the
play's constant themes: self-knowledge. Moscón is led to see
himself (and to confess it aloud) for what he is; the false blind
man and his shady companions are not. Florindo and Braulio see
the error of their ways; Pelagio does not.

In this thematic thread that unifies the work, Ildefonso's
case calls for special comment. At the end of the action, Ildefonso comes to value and accept his service to Mary as extra-
ordinary. Whereas in the more common end to Ildefonso's story,
the saint is allowed to continue, humbly, to serve Mary for a
while yet on earth, Valdivielso permits his protagonist to understand that he is exceptional (thus the equation with Moses), that
he has been to the mountaintop and glimpsed Heaven, and likens
his return to the secular world (the crowd awaiting him outside
the Cathedral) to the descent from Sinai with its accompanying
joyous news.

Doubtless, Valdivielso is writing at a moment in history that
requires a certain magnification of all that affects Toledo. He
had done it in his *Sagrario* and he repeats the performance here.
While the self-appraisal by Ildefonso is consonant with his character in the *Descensión*, and with the underlying theme of self-
knowledge, it is, so far as I know, an element original with this
telling of the Ildefonso story.

Another original element seems to be the introduction of the
vieja. She is feisty and militant but, also, a bit of a sleepy-
head. Having fallen asleep in the Cathedral saying her rosary,
she is startled awake when an angel is placing candles on the altar. She is allowed to receive a candle herself, but breaks her
promise to return it later when it comes to symbolize the potent
miracle she has unwittingly been a passive witness to. Her wish--
to keep the candle to the hour of her death--is granted with no
rancor on the part of the understanding angel. Since there are
no stage directions to the contrary, the play ends a few moments
later, the *vieja* still on stage with the transfigured Ildefonso.

The long final scene--through which the old woman catnaps--
has been carefully led up to. Leocadia, for example, has said
that Mary would like to visit (576-83). The blind man expresses
his desire that Leocadia's intimations of such a divine visit come
to fruition (953-56). But Valdivielso had also been preparing for
the scene: some of the heaviest borrowing from the *Sagrario de Toledo* reappears in this scene. Good examples of Valdivielso's
sustained poetry occur in two noteworthy sequences here, in the
two soliloquies between lines 1224 and 1319 and in the speeches
accompanying the investiture of the *casulla* (1343-66).

3, VALDIVIELSO'S DRAMATIC ART

Earlier (p. XI) I emphasized that Valdivielso put some special efforts into this play. While its merits are many, I have chosen
four of the areas which seem to me to prove that his efforts paid
handsome artistic dividends: characterization; use of image pattern-
ing; anticipation-presentation-recapitulation sequences; and versification.

A fine example of the first area is the figure of Moscón, whose
name in thieves' cant means one who, feigning ignorance, wins
through to his goal (*Dicc. Aut.* 2:614). The other characters often mock his name (890, 905-06) and seem to be alert to his taste

for verbal thrust and parry, joining him in it only too willingly.
He is too clever by half: feeling privileged to be in service to
a fine family, he is quick to presume that he has placed himself
out of his social class (157-62). The manifestation of this can
be hilarious when Moscón is speaking his heavily hispanicized
Latin, as he often does. His job is to distribute Ildefonso's
largesse to the poor, but he is caught reserving some for himself (1206) or declaring the soup spilled and not available (888).
He habitually postures as a tough guy (170-72, 194-97) but his
vaunted fearlessness can rapidly disappear when real dangers
threaten, earthly (907-12) and divine (1203-09). As is expected
of one who is trained to live by his self-(mis)representation,
Moscón does possess great verbal wit. His repartee is sharp, his
asides cutting (990-91), and he is author of the cleverest joke
in the text (960-67) as he exchanges earthly words with Ildefonso.

The unintentionally humorous metaphor employed at line 256
becomes a deft stroke of characterization, as does his hurt feeling at the *vieja's* criticism of his garbled latinizing. We see
him as cynical, selfish, and sly in one context, but the selfless
retainer, curious, likable, and human in another. In fine, Moscón
is a well worked out creation who engages, notwithstanding our
recognition of all his human weaknesses, our sympathy and understanding. He endears himself to the reader and is one of the
nice surprises in the enlarged cast of characters we might expect
in a new treatment of the Ildefonso story.

For an example of artistic use of an image pattern there is
much to select from. I will explore the one that appears in the
opening line of the play. Florindo, the heretic, is appealing
to night to spread out her "lobuna capa" in order to aid in the
concealment of Pelagio from forces in close pursuit. "Lobuna"
suggests the equation of "night" with "wolf" and the ideas of
stealth and secrecy reinforce the association. In the cant of
the day, "lobuna" was applied to thieves and other scoundrels

who work their evil under cover of night (*Dicc. Aut.* 2: 427-28).
Florindo's speech goes on to extend this protection to "lamias"
(15) and to "escaladores" (18) who thrive in darkness and revile
the light of day.

The wolf is also the traditional enemy of the shepherd (Ildefonso) and the initial adjective describing the night which will
conceal the heretic seems particularly well chosen. The wolf,
like Pelagio, hides in lairs and caves (40). When heretics venture
into the light, they choose disguise (Florindo and Braulio as
pilgrims, Pelagio as a farmer), for else they would--like wolves--
be subject to stoning (80-88, 167).

The music sung at 267-68 ("Los herejes lobos / huyen del pastor") further identifies the heretics as wolves, but cleverly also
identifies them as former sheep (the meaning, at another level, of
"hereje lobo"). This reading is supported later when Florindo and
Braulio turn themselves over to Ildefonso, Braulio saying:

> De entre çarças del error
> del lobo infernal heridas,
> estas ovejas perdidas
> vuelven a su buen Pastor. (741-44)

The second of these quoted lines makes the ideological split with
their unrepentant leader, Pelagio, definitive. They can call him
"infernal": their return is complete. This important difference
between Pelagio, on the one hand, and Braulio and Florindo on the
other, is further underscored in the scene in which Pelagio must
come face to face with the Angel of Justice.

Just as the earth is about to open and swallow up Pelagio, the
Angel stands above him, lance poised for the fatal thrust (its i-
conographic similarity to St. Michael poised above Satan in the
Book of Revelations not to be missed), and speaks:

> ¡Cai en el laço que armaste!
> ¡Cai en la cueva que hiçiste! (1080-81)

The "cueva" becomes the dark hole of the wolf's lair into which the sinner now will be eternally imprisoned; but it is also sign and symbol of his internal emptiness and of his punishment: the black pit of Hell. Having rejected bona fide offers of forgiveness (1066-69), Pelagio must now lie in the bed of his own making.

The "lobuna"-tinged imagery throughout the play helps to give literary shape and definition to the heretics. It also assists, as we have seen, in differentiating among them, at least with reference to repentance and forgiveness. One, Pelagio, turns out to have been a wolf in wolf's clothing while it turns out that the repentant duo were really lambs all along, only momentarily led astray.

The third area in which Valdivielso demonstrates artistic foresight is in the way in which he anticipates an action, then presents it, and, finally, harkens back to it. In this area, the Leocadia scenes are outstanding examples. She appears only the one time. In spite of this, we know she is anticipated at line 280 when the king sets out for the mass in her honor (the lines belong to Moscón) and again, twice, Leocadia is anticipated by the heretics, Florindo and Braulio (309-12, 431-34). The anticipation is heightened by the direct allusions to Leocadia in the off-stage music even before the miracle occurs:

> A Leocadia Ylefonso / pide con ruego,
>
> que la parte de tierra / descubre el Cielo. (468-71)

It seems almost a *fait accompli*, despite its still being anticipated, when the king himself implores that Leocadia's true resting place be revealed (476-81).

The anticipation ends when Leocadia emerges from the tomb. Yet when she returns there, her action finished, she does not disppear altogether from the hearts and minds of the players on the stage and this scene is recalled time and again. A page recalls the sights and sounds of the miraculous evening for Moscón who was not present (745ff). The false blind man (at 870ff

and 948-52) commisions a *romance de ciego* to record those happen-
ings. Florindo recalls the scene (1014-15) and the old woman la-
ments having had to miss it even while she is regaling   her lis-
teners with a second-hand account of the events (1132-47).

Thus, even in the scenes which mediate the two visits from
the divine representatives, the first of them, Leocadia, is still
being recalled in widening ripples of memory affecting almost all
of the characters, even those who were not witness to the miracle.
This cycle, with its own rhythmic movement from anticipation to
presentation and on to recapitulation, may be seen collectively
as part of the anticipation scheme for the moment of final apotheosis, the confirmation of Ildefonso's stature as saint, chosen, and
saved.

The final area in which Valdivieso exerts special dramatic ex-
pertise is versification. It is well known that in the overall
verse production of Valdivielso, the octava reigns supreme.[19] His
long verse epics on St. Joseph and the *Sagrario de Toledo* use that
stanza and versification scheme exclusively, as do many occasional
pieces dispersed among his writings. Far greater range is evident
in his theatre, however, as the following charts will show for the
Descensión. In this piece, there are 1416 lines of verse. My
edition numbers lines that are split between two speakers: this
accounts for the difference between the 1479 lines numbered in the
text and the total number of verses in the chart below, which is
arranged sequentially to show the frequency of versification change
(23 times). I chose the scene boundaries (none are marked in the
autograph of Roxas) to suit my sense of the flow of the play's action, and this has resulted, I hope not disturbingly, in some scenes
being linked by versification schemes (5 and 6, 12 and 13 by *redondillas*; 10 and 11 by a *romance* in í-o).

Lines	Strophic form/type	Syll/line	Scene	Total lines
1-69	romance (ó-e)	8	1	68
70-78	cuartetas (2)	8	2	8
80-201	romance (í-a)	8	2-3	112
203-42	octavas (5)	11	4	40
243-66	romance (á-o)	8	5	24
267-70	romancillo (ó)	6	5	4
271-76	romance (ó)	8	5	6
277-78	romancillo (ó)	6	5	2
279-434	redondillas (37)	8	5-6	148
435-67	verso libre	11	7-8	29
468-71	seguidilla (1)	7 5	8	2 2
472-91	décimas (2)	8	8	20
492-95	romancillo (é-a)	6*	8	4
496-668	romance (ó-a)	8	8	172
669-72	romancillo (é-a)	6*	8	4
673-744	redondillas (18)	8	9	72
745-72	verso libre	11	10	27
773-1021	romance (í-o)	8	10-11	232
1022-1159	redondillas (33)	8	12-13	132
1160-1219	verso libre	11	13	56
1220-1223	seguidilla (1)	7 5	14	2 2
1224-1342	romance (á-e)	8	14	116
1343-1366	octavas (3)	11	14	24
1367-1370	cuarteto (1)	10	14	4
1371-1479	octavas (13)	11	14	104

The following notes and comments are meant to supplement the information in the table above. The *seguidillas, romancillos,* and *cuartetas* noted are employed exclusively in musical interventions and, thus, comment on the developing action rather than advance it in any significant way. This means that the remainder of the play in composed in a variety of octosyllabic and hendeca-

syllabic verse forms. The preeminence of these forms is clearly
shown in the following table.

METER	LINES	PER CENT
Octosyllables (*romance, décima, cuarteta, redondilla*)	1,100	78.40
Hendecasyllables (*octava, verso libre*)	280	19.77
Hexasyllables (*romancillo*)	14	.99
Decasyllables (*1367-70*)	4	.28
Heptasyllables (*seguidilla*)	4	.28
Pentasyllables (*seguidilla*)	4	.28

The *romances*, with 730 lines of verse, are about half of the total, while the other popular octosyllabic form of the *Descensión*,
the *redondilla*, take up about one quarter of the total lines. The
two *décimas* are used in an exchange between the king and Ildefonso,
and seem to underscore the respectful treatment each reserves for
the other.

The resonant *octavas*, with one exception (1436-47), are used
only by Ildefonso and the Virgin, and capture the loving relationship they share. The interplay between the remaining characters
and the narrative expositions are largely carried on the *romance*
and the *redondilla*. For example, Florindo's play-opening appeal
to night (1-49), Leocadia's message to Ildefonso and the assembled
devout (496-588), and the Virgin's opening speech (1224-87) are
all in *romance* meter; Pelagio's unrepentant statements--and the
Angel's response--at the time of Pelagio's condemnation (1022-93),
and the *vieja*'s revelation of her love for Mary (1112-59) are ver-
sified in *redondillas*.

The free verse hendecasyllables are used on three separate
occasions, in transitional and heavily expository scenes: the discussion between the soldiers and the populace before the Leocadia
appearance (435-67); a recapitulation of this miracle later (745-
72); and the conversation of Moscón and the sacristan when Moscón
is led to his confessions (1160-1219).

The alternation of verse forms and their variety invest the play with what must be seen as a design to match verse to mood. The *romance*, used on six different occasions, has as many assonance patterns (see the table, p. XXVI). The final series of free verse lines are often divided between two characters, emphasizing a certain snappiness in the dialogue and lightening the weight of the hendecasyllables at the same time. Ildefonso, seen juxtaposed in action or dialogue with most all of the characters, is capable of responding to all in the same verse form as is used with him, a usage which underscores the active characterization of the saint as a man for all the people.

All of this seems to be in general accord with standard poly-metric usage in the early seventeenth century. It is here applied with skill, grace, and mastery of speech rhythms. It confers to the flow of dialogue a certain elasticity and variation which is pleasant, and a wide range of expression for the changes in tone and mood recorded throughout, ending only with the stately *octavas* between Ildefonso and his Heavenly Queen and with a suspension of the highest tone achieved as Ildefonso, caught in ecstasy, turns his thought once again earthward.

4. VALDIVIELSO, LOPE, AND THE 'CERTAMEN POETICO' OF 1616

In 1616, at the time of the *certamen poético* celebrating the restoration of the chapel of the Virgen del Sagrario, Valdivielso and Lope had long been friends. It was, of course, a literary as well as a personal friendship since they were almost equally prolific in at least one sense: "El maestro José de Valdivielso es el único escritor de los Siglos de Oro que puede competir en prodigalidad con Lope de Vega respecto a escritos publicados en obras de otros autores, bien como censuras o elogios de los preliminares, bien como piezas remitidas a justas o certámenes."[20]

Lope paid high tribute to his friend in 1604 in a poem he composed for Valdivielso's *Vida de San José*, with a sonnet, "Joseph

canta a Joseph, Joseph humano." The was the year when Lope tempo-
rarily moved to Toledo and their friendship deepened. Both men
belonged to some of the by-then depleted ranks of the literary
academies that still met in Toledo (the new groups in Madrid had
attracted many writers to the court). There they met with other
Toledo-based men of note, among them Baltasar Eliseo de Medinilla,
Tomás Tamayo de Vargas, Francisco de Céspedes, Martín Chacón, Francisco de Pisa, Alfonso de Contreras, and, on occasion, el Greco.[21]

Valdivielso in 1605 baptized Marcela, the daughter Lope had
with Micaela de Luján, although Lope now only sporadically visited
Toledo. They met in Madrid, too, for Valdivielso accompanied the
archbishop to Philip's court on many occasions. Valdivielso's
visits to Madrid were especially frequent after 1609, at a time
when Lope and his partisans were the dominant force at court and
exerted a strong influence on acceptable tastes in literary output.
In the previous year--1608--Lope had returned to Toledo to master-
mind the poetic contests for the Holy Sacrament. It was for Lope
a great personal triumph, but it may also have played an ironic
role in stimulating Luis de Góngora to master Lope's organizational
procedures and to begin planning to have--in some as yet unspecified
future--his own day in the sun at Lope's expense. And this is pre-
cisely what happened in 1616.[22]

Other factors were leading up to this same end. Despite his
chaplain's friendship with Lope, the Cardinal-Archbishop Sandoval
y Rojas was no partisan of el Fénix. There seemed always to be
tension between them, not lessened at all by the fact that in 1614
the archbishop, under pressure from Lope's influential protector,
the Duke of Sessa, administered Lope's final vows. It seems most
likely that when in 1616 the archbishop was planning the festivities for the new chapel of the Virgen del Sagrario, he desired to
exclude Lope and took advantage of growing tensions between him
and the Cordoban Góngora to further that goal.[23]

These tensions between the two poet rivals had been intensified in 1613. It was the strong belief of Góngora, and of his

vocal group of supporters, that Lope was chiefly responsible for the criticism aimed at two of the former's works, *Polífemo* and the *Soledades*, then circulating in manuscript. Lope probably did serve as captain of a group of literati hostile to the new wave of poetry of which Góngora was the chief exponent. Earlier, in a sonnet also circulated in manuscript, Lope had seemed to praise his Cordoban rival;[24] however, as that rival gained adherents and advocates, some even at court, Lope may well have taken the defensive by encouraging his followers to strike back. In the next few years, it seemed that Lope's star was on the wane, and the bitterness of the invective exchanged between the two groups of strongly partisan poets increased in shrillness.

At the time of the *certamen poético* held in Toledo in 1616, the friar Hortensio Félix Paravicino--later a friend of Lope's-- was counted in the camp of Lope's rival Góngora. How Sandoval y Rojas used this fact to exclude Lope will appear clear from the following:

> La llegada de Góngora a Madrid en 1617 se anunció por
> un triunfo previo de la poesía culta (...) [E]l Certamen
> Poético celebrado en Toledo, en octubre de 1616 . . . se
> organizó bajo la alta protección del cardenal Sandoval y
> Rojas, que hizo construir la capilla [del Sagrario], pu-
> blicándose en el palacio arzobispal y en Madrid, en la
> casa del cardenal, con un cartel de fray Hortensio Fé-
> lix de Paravicino, el cual, capitaneando a los parti-
> darios de Góngora, preparó aquella Justa Poética para
> lucimiento del gran lírico cordobés, quien presentó a
> ella sus bellísimas octavas reales "Al favor que San
> Ildefonso recibió de Nuestra Señora."
>
>   No concurrieron por esto al certamen ni Lope de
> Vega ni sus amigos íntimos, como Elíseo de Medinilla
> --que aun vivía--y Tamayo de Vargas, quienes, toledanos
> y aficionados a esta clase de fiestas, estaban casi

> obligados a asistir (...) En cambio, tomaron parte
> en él los enemigos de Lope: Suárez de Figueroa y
> Torres Rámila, con Cristóbal de Mesa y don Esteban
> Manuel de Villegas,[25] que así se reunían al mayor
> rival del poeta madrileño... .[26]

Not only did Sandoval y Rojas place Paravicino deliberately in
this position to irritate Lope and his partisans, but he must also
have made his chaplain acutely uncomfortable by making him serve
as secretary of the *certamen*, an assignment he was in no position
to refuse. That the Cardinal's attempt to exclude Lope was even
more successful than already indicated by the account given above
is obvious from another fact. Of the members of the Count of
Fuensalida's literary academy listed for us by Marañón (see n.
21), about a third took active part in the Justa Poética for the
Holy Sacrament, organized by Lope in 1608, or in another he organized in 1605, also celebrated in Toledo. Only two of this number
saw fit to try their skills in the 1616 competition, and one of
these was Valdivielso who, as we have seen, had little choice. In
this light, then, we may see that events and personalities conspired to deal Lope a (temporary) setback in his literary fortunes
in 1616, even as Góngora, preparing his triumphant conquest of the
Madrid court for 1617, stung by what he believed to be Lope's role
in holding back his career, was a willing participant in his rival's humiliation.

    The Góngora-Lope rivalry is detailed elsewhere and we need not
explore it any further here.[27] But what has been given so far is
necessary to a fuller comprehension of yet another complicated
relationship--that of Lope's *comedia de santo, El capellán de la
Virgen*, with its vitriolic parody of *culterano* poetry, and Joseph
de Valdivielso's *Descensión de la Virgen*. We can state with some
precision when the latter play was written; however, for Lope's
play, there are only estimations of the date of composition (it
did not appear in printed form until the XVIII Parte of 1623). The
best guesses are that it dates from after 1613, the year Góngora's

Polifemo and *Soledades* began circulating and came to the attention
of Lope de Vega. How early or late after that time we cannot say
for sure. I think it likely that it may have been close to the
time of the *certamen poético* from which Lope had so deliberately
been excluded.

Up until that time Lope had occasionally made his home in Toledo. Many of his friends lived and worked there. He organized
poetry contests there in 1605 and 1608. It may be of especial interest to note that in the 1608 competition Lope himself entered
a sonnet, "Cuelgan racimos de ángeles, que enrizan," on the theme
of the descent of the Virgin to honor Ildefonso, the same theme
which would be so prominent in the celebrations of 1616. But now
his adversary would have the honor of entering the competition
and producing a poem written in the new style. And this practi-
cally in Lope's own back yard, so to speak. While this series of
events may not have prompted the writing of Lope's *Capellán*, it
nevertheless seems certain that the incorporation of the sonnet
parody (which could have been penned earlier, and perhaps even
circulated independently in manuscript among the faithful) into
the play makes such a time frame logical. A reference to Lope's
sonnet in 1617 makes that year the *terminus ad quem* for the composition of his Ildefonso play.

The psychological moment provided Lope by the events of 1616
has convinced others, too, that the triumph of the *culterano*
style (Góngora did take first prize for his Ildefonso poem) must
be contemporaneous with the writing of *El capellán*:

> Evidentemente il Fenix non poté fare a meno, dato il
> clima politico-religioso che ben conosciamo, di portare
> in teatro il "gran defensor de la inmaculada pureza de
> la Emperatriz del Cielo, Nuestra Señora," como lo de-
> finisce nella dedica della commedia,[28]

and

> . . .a la sazón [Lope] se hallaba escribiendo su comedia
> *El capellán de la Virgen*, [e] intercaló en ella una es-

cena graciosísima en la que, con un soneto, carica-
turizaba el estilo de la llamada nueva poesía, de la
que era paladín Góngora.[29]

The author of these last lines, Sainz de Robles, believes further
that the success of Lope's sonnet satire led Góngora to write a
letter in which he accused Lope of being "hereje y alumbrado,"[30]
after which the real war between the two gained new momentum.
Joaquín de Entrambasaguas who has looked into this rivalry with
great care, agrees that Lope was preparing El capellán to celebrate the upcoming commemoration of the descent of Mary to the
Cathedral of Toledo; he believes, however, that the work was under
way when Lope saw how the winds had shifted--to Góngora-- and he
chose to respond with the sonnet, which he decided to incorporate
into the play.[31] Millé counters with his idea that Lope took up
the writing of his play as a response to the Cardinal's actions.[32]

   In essence, all of these scholars fix on 1616 as the date when
Lope most probably wrote his Ildefonso play. The likelihood that
they are right is strong. But not everyone concurs. For example,
Morley-Bruerton place the composition slightly earlier, in 1614
or 1615, but adduce no supporting evidence.[33] I believe that a
case can be made for the earlier dates they suggest. The point,
while it may not be resolved here, is certainly worth stating in
full: I suspect that Valdivielso's Descensión may have been in
part inspired by Lope's El capellán. If Lope was writing it in
1616, it seems unlikely that Valdivielso could have made much use
of it. If Valdivielso does draw upon Lope's Ildefonso play, then
it surely must have been known to him earlier. I intend to explore this whole matter at length elsewhere, but should like to
outline the arguments at this juncture, since they would have been
pure conjecture without the text of the Descensión, largely unavail-
able until now.

   It could have happened as follows. The attention focussed on
Ildefonso was notable in Lope's time. In the mid-sixteenth century, Toledo had unsuccessfully pursued a suit to have the mortal

remains of Ildefonso returned to his native city from Zamora, where they had been revered since their modern re-discovery in 1260. Then there were, in 1565 and 1587 respectively, the return to Toledo of the remains of two saints intimately connected with the story of Ildefonso, Eugenio III (Ildefonso's uncle and predecessor as archbishop), and Leocadia. On each of these occasions Ildefonso was paid tribute in the sermons, services, and literary exercises devised for the solemn festivities honoring other Toledan saints.

In 1602 Philip III went in pilgrimage to Zamora to adore the relics of Ildefonso. The travellers of the *Viaje entretenido* of 1603 invite readers to ponder the fame acquired for Toledo in the great favor bestowed on it when the Virgin descended to present Ildefonso with the chasuble. Work on the new chapel which will house the Virgen del Sagrario is under way when Lope, along with twenty-one others pen their sonnets to the miraculous descent of divinity at the 1608 *certamen poético*, mentioned above, in honor of the Holy Sacrament.[34] Lope's close ties with Toledo and with Valdivielso, from 1604--when he first took up residence there-- until later would have permitted him many opportunities to work extensively with the Ildefonso story. One period in particular might be after 1609, the year Valdivielso came often to Madrid, and extending until 1616, a time when, as was noted earlier, Valdivielso was at work on his *Sagrario de Toledo*. One further and related possibility seems warranted in this sequence of events. Lope, knowing of the great work on the chapel that was of some moment in the life of the Cardinal whose opposition to him was not so lightly masked at times, and cognizant of the pressures under which this Cardinal administered--in 1614--his final vows, may have undertaken to write his Ildefonso play in the belief that it might gain him some better standing in the Cardinal's eyes.

Be that as it may, this must remain in the realm of speculation. Lope, before the events of 1614, had already made known his opinion of the new style in poetry being championed by Góngora. He wrote, in fact, to his mentor, the Duke of Sessa, a let-

ter which was most bitter in its references to the Cordoban poet
and certain of his followers, among them Paravicino. Is it not
possible that Lope, having conceived and written (some, if not all)
his *Capellán* in this period, inserted his bitter sonnet previous
to the triumph of Góngora in the 1616 *certamen poético*? I would
submit that it was possible, if we can safely place the composition
of the play at this earlier period.

Lending some credence to this theory of early composition for
the *Capellán de la Virgen* (and its anti-Góngora sonnet) is the fact
that the offending sonnet--replete with the odious transpositions
Lope and his group loved to hate--has no specific allusions to the
contents of the *octavas* Góngora composed for the poetic jousts of
October, 1616. This in contrast with the use of specific lines
from those *octavas* in Lope's *Papel de la nueva poesía*, published
in 1621.[35]

A final point brings us back to Valdivielso and the *Descensión*.
Lope was certainly aware that his friend had been busy creating, in
spare moments, an epic poem on Ildefonso. Work on it had begun no
later than 1612 and I think it plausible that parts of this work
had been discussed by the two poets. Furthermore, it seems likely
that Valdivielso had shown his friend some of the manuscript during
the years before the first printing of the *Sagrario* in 1616. Such
strong probabilities reinforce my feeling that Lope did not need
the events of the *certamen poético* to encourage him to hone his
talents with the Ildefonso play. On the contrary, there are parts
of the *Descensión* text that make me a partisan of the opposing view:
Lope had written his *Capellán* earlier.

If Valdivielso, writing his play in 1616, drew on his own manuscript of the *Sagrario*, he seems also to have drawn on Lope, too,
for inspiration. The interesting possibility that occurs to me is
that Lope, having nurtured some of his thoughts about the shape of
the Ildefonso story in discussion with his friend, Valdivielso,
wrote his play sometime around 1614 following designs of his own.
Valdivielso will have read Lope's play in manuscript and later will

witness its zest--particularly in the creation of the comic cha1
ters--stealing into his *Descensión*.

If Lope's play is not late 1616 or 1617, it does not seem tc
likely that it was written in early 1616 either. By La Barrera'
account Lope was detained in Valencia until early September of
1616, by which time the *certamen* had been organized and proclaim
by the archbishop.[36] Valdivielso, in drawing on Lope's *Capellán*
would have been doing exactly what he did when he drew from his
friend's *El villano en su rincón* for an *auto* of the same name.

We have seen that Valdivielso "borrowed" *octavas* from his ow
Sagrario in the dramatization of the religious scenes in the *Des
censión*. The other story line, which portrays the common folk
of Toledo--the rabble, the charlatans, and the humble--wears a
distinctive Lopean dress. Readers of both plays will note the
strong resemblance of the opening scenes of Valdivielso's play
with the following scene from *El capellán de la Virgen*. Nuño and
Mendo --in the roles of Moscón and the street urchins--take to
the streets, armed with clubs and with the desire to break open
the heads of all who will not proclaim the purity of the Virgin.

In another scene from Lope, Ildefonso is speaking in private
with Braulio (as in Valdivielso, the name of one of the heretics
when they are interrupted by Ramiro, a servant of the archbishop
who desires to know what they are speaking of so earnestly. Ilde
fonso rebukes Ramiro thus:

> *Utrum homines*, *habemus*
> tratado, Ramiro amigo;
> *assumantur* fue el sujeto
> *ad ordines Angelorum*. (p. 282)

Is it not possible, given my earlier speculations on the
prior   (ca. 1614) composition of Lope's play, that we can seek
in these and similar passages of *El Capellán* the germ of Valdivielso's decision to endow the crafty Moscón with his blend of
Latin and the vernacular (criticized by the sacristan and the
vieja), in his attempt to imitate the speech of his master, the

archbishop Ildefonso (from Lope?). While these two plays--so close in time and theme--are so differently motivated, the Lopean overtones in the Valdivielso play are quite strong and deserve more attention than they can receive here.

It is time to conclude these speculative remarks. While no really new hard evidence has been produced in recent years to help fix the date of the composition of Lope's play, it is my suggestion that the text of Valdivielso's *Descensión* may be another part of the puzzle and, possibly, it may offer a clue to its solution. The prevailing notion (Millé, Entrambasaguas, etc.) is that Lope took up his pen as a consequence of Góngora's triumph in the *certamen poético* of 1616, an event that most certainly was conceived to upstage Lope in favor of his rival. My notion is that, having looked at the pattern of the friendship and literary association of Lope and Valdivielso, having grafted the *Descensión* onto that pattern, and having probed the possibilities of earlier circumstances producing conditions ripe for Lope's play *and its anti-Góngora sonnet*, Lope could easily have written his Ildefonso play in 1614 or early 1615, as suggested by Morley-Bruerton without supporting arguments.

If I am right and this reconstruction of events is correct, or nearly correct, then it gives belated pleasure to the reader of the *Descensión* to imagine that Valdivielso assuages some of his personal discomfort at having to perform as secretary of events, and to write plays for presentation at festivities from which his friend Lope was rather curtly excluded, by transforming parts of *El capellán de la Virgen* into the life of his own *Descensión* and passing it under the noses of the very people who had worked so hard to see Lope banished--in person and in spirit--from the literary events marking the grand occasion.

5. ABOUT THIS EDITION

Two manuscript copies of this play exist. Both are located in Madrid, in the Sección de Raros of the Biblioteca Nacional. The earlier and more reliable of the two copies dates from 1643 in an autograph copy of Francisco de Roxas, himself a playwright and a friend of Valdivielso. The second copy has the name "Lanini" written on the title page and is written in a characteristically eighteenth-century hand. The flaws in this copy include omissions (lines 123, 834, to cite but two examples), lines written in reverse order, lines which are made metrically awkward by interpolations, and the like. There are, too, signs of hurried copying: excessive abbreviation, a partial list of characters, and unclear writing (although very few words are, from context, hard to ascertain). Much of the latinizing that Moscón is responsible for has been re-hispanicized, thus altering the characterization of the archbishop's employee. While these faults may derive from an earlier copy, it is clear that the significant variants (see, for example, the discussion in the note to line 1086) show that it was not the 1643 copy that was used for this later text.

Nor do we know what copy Roxas copied from. Was it one that he had obtained from its author? Was it in such shape that a new copying was deemed necessary to its preservation? Was it being prepared for publication posthumously, perhaps as a friend's last tribute? Whatever the reasons behind the newly produced copy, Roxas prepared it with great care for legibility and metrical regularity. What small interventions might be the work of Roxas we can never know, barring the appearance of a Valdivielso autograph. Still, I think the circumstances of friendship, in view of the clarity of the copy and the obvious care that went into its preparation, argue for a faithful text.

In editing, I have attempted to produce a readable format which retains all the flavor of the original. A few emendations, largely restoration of missing letters, have been made: these are indicated by parentheses. I have adopted the common editorial practice of assigning fixed vowel and consonant values to the 'u' and 'v' and of transcribing initial 'rr' as 'R'. I have, in addition, adopted modern orthographical standards for the 'h'; thus, 'aya' becomes 'haya' and 'hecho' becomes 'echó' (on one occasion).

Abbreviations are resolved silently throughout. I have respected modern word boundaries (one exception: dél) and adopted modern practices in capitalization and accentuation. Punctuation in the copy is inconsistent and does not always provide a clear reading; thus, I have punctuated according to contemporary usage, striving always for clarity. My own additions are limited to: the creation of scene divisions, the numbering of lines in the text, the proper placement of the stage directions, and the notation in the right margin of the folio numbers of the Roxas copy of the *Descensión*.

I have, with the exceptions noted above, respected spelling variants (dotrina/doctrina, pecado/peccado, cual/qual, verla/vella, im-/in-, and so forth) and allowed the i/y and j/g alternations to stand. The result is a text which is faithful to the 1643 original while conforming to most of the accepted editorial practices in common use for the presentation of seventeenth-century Spanish texts. Both the scholar and the student approaching the text for the first time are the potential readers of the *Auto* and I have tried to respect the needs of both groups.

NOTES TO THE INTRODUCTION

1. An interesting dimension of the opulent festivities in the
Toledo of 1616 is that both Santiago de Compostela and Sevilla
were pressing claims to the title of Primate Church of Spain.
The events of October and November—designed by Sandoval y
Rojas to emphasize the claims of Toledo—were in part a strong
response to such rival cities. See, for example, Tomás Tamayo
y Vargas, *Defensa de la Descensión de la Virgen Nuestra Señora
a la Santa Iglesia de Toledo a dar la casulla a su B. capellán
San Ilefonso* (Toledo: Diego Rodríguez, 1616), which was printed
in July and dedicated to the Cardinal-Archbishop.

2. For biographical details on Valdivielso, consult J. M. Aguirre,
José de Valdivielso y la poesía religiosa tradicional (Toledo:
Inst. Provincial de Investigaciones y Estudios Toledanos, 1965),
chapter 1, or Ricardo Arias, *The Spanish Sacramental Plays* (Boston: Twayne, 1980), 111-121.

3. See. P. Miguel Hernández, *Vida, Martyrio y Translación de la
gloriosa Virgen y Mártyr Santa Leocadia...1587* (Toledo, 1591).

4. Sandoval y Rojas, fittingly, was buried in this chapel, with
which construction he is closely identified. Tirso de Molina,
in *No hay peor sordo,* recalls the event: "Trofeos ha levantado/
donde los pies estampó/ la que honrando la cogulla/ del santo
que a España medra,/imprimió su fama en piedra/ y le dio inmortal casulla."

5. See Pedro de Herrera, *Descripción de la Capilla de Nuestra Señora del Sagrario* (Madrid: Luis Sánchez, 1617).

6. In 1602, Philip and his queen, Margaret of Austria, had made a
pilgrimage to Zamora where, on February 15-19, the mortal remains of Ildefonso were displayed. Later, in 1619, when Philip
was dangerously ill, Ildefonso's relics were paraded through
the streets of Zamora as a supplication for the heavenly favor
of the return of the monarch's health. See E. Fernández-Prieto
Domínguez, *Actas de visitas reales y otras realizadas por acontecimientos extraordinarios a los cuerpos de San Ildefonso y
San Atilano, años 1462-1960* (Zamora: Tip. Heraldo de Zamora, 1973).

7. On the *auto's* charming blend of sacred and profane characters
and scenes, "durent plaire singulièrement au public réuni sur
la place del Ayuntamiento" (Rouanet, p. 59).

8. This quotation appears in Herrera's *Descripción de la Capilla* (see above, note 5) as the concluding paragraph to the "Introdución" (pp. 17-18).

9. See A. Braegelman, *The Life and Writings of Saint Ildefonsus of Toledo* (Washington, D.C.: The Catholic Univ. of America Press, 1942); A. Custodio Vega, "De patrología española: San Ildefonso de Toledo, sus biografías y sus biógrafos. Y sus *Varones ilustres*," *Bol. de la Real Ac. de la Hist.*, 145 (1969), 35-107; and J. M. Canal, "San Hildefonso de Toledo, historia y leyenda," *Ephemerides Mariologicae*, 17 (1967), 437-462.

10. The best edition is Vicente Blanco García, *San Ildefonso. 'De virginitate beatae Mariae': historia de su tradición manuscrita, texto y comentario gramatical y estilístico* (Madrid, 1937).

11. José Madoz, "San Ildefonso de Toledo," *Estudios eclesiásticos*, 26 (1952), 467-505; see especially pp. 488-495.

12. Whether there was a similar heresy in Ildefonso's time seems to be in some doubt (see the works in n. 9, above). The devout of later centuries certainly did not question its historicity.

13. Early examples are included in the illuminations of MS 10087 of the Biblioteca Nacional in Madrid.

14. One example of a change surfaces in the sixteenth century, in a *romance* in Juan López de Ubeda's *Cancionero y vergel de plantas divinas* (Alcalá, 1588). I give the first eight lines: "Armando están caballero/ a Ildefonso toledano,/ en el templo de la Virgen/ en un altar soberano./ Arnés tranzado le visten,/ hermoso, rico y dorado;/ con la sobrevesta roja,/ yelmo y plumas va galano."

15. The best known depiction of this scene is the large canvas by Pedro Orrente, in the cathedral of Toledo. The Prado owns an eighteenth-century relief sculpture by Robert Michel.

16. Murillo's much-praised canvas, in the Prado, is the best known of these. Rubens' version is at Vienna's Kunsthistorisches Museum and Velázquez's is in Seville. I know of over sixty other painted "imposiciones."

17. See D. Devoto, "Tres notas sobre Berceo y la historia eclesiástica española. I: Alba o casulla; ofrenda," *Bulletin Hispanique*, 70 (1968), 261-287.

18. A special chapel houses this stone today. It was built by Alonso de Fonseca sometime before 1603. For an indication of its fame, see Rojas Villandrando's *Viaje entretenido* (ed. J. P. Ressot, Madrid: Castalia, 1972, pp. 281-282).

19. A recent statement says that Valdivielso's works are "siempre en verso, en verso abundante, generoso, torrencial a veces y,

casi sin excepción, en inacabables tiradas de octavas reales"
(F. Allué y Morer, "Centenario de un poeta: el Mro. Joseph de
Valdivielso," *Poesía española*, Second Series, no. 90 [June,
1960], p. 22). Criticism is of the long epic poems.

20. J. Simón Díaz, "Textos dispersos de clásicos españoles, XI:
Valdivielso," *Revista de literatura*, 19 (1961), 125.

21. Consult Gregorio Marañón, *El Greco y Toledo* (Madrid: Espasa-
Calpe, 1956), pp. 91-102.

22. J. Entrambasaguas, *Lope de Vega en las Justas Poéticas toledanas de 1605 y 1608* (Madrid, 1969), p. 18.

23. "No es dudoso que la organización de esta justa envolvía un
ataque más o menos directa contra Lope y su escuela" (G. Millé
y Giménez, "El papel de la nueva poesía [Lope, Góngora y los
orígenes del culteranismo]," in *Estudios de literatura española* (La Plata, Argentina: Fac. de Letras y Ciencias de Educación, 1928), p. 196.

24. The sonnet was not printed until 1621 in *La Filomena*.

25. For a more extensive list of the participants, see C. Pérez
Pastor, *Bibliografía madrileña de los siglos XVI-XVII, Vol.
II: 1601-1620* (Madrid, 1906; rpt. Amsterdam: Van Heusden,
1971), 409-410.

26. J. Entrambasaguas, *Lope de Vega y su tiempo*, I (Barcelona:
Teide, 1961), p. 130.

27. See the works cited in notes 22, 23, and 26. See also the more
recent study of Ana Martínez Arancón, *La batalla en torno a
Góngora* (Barcelona: A. Bosch, 1978).

28. Elisa Aragone Terni, *Studio sulle "comedias de santo" di Lope
de Vega* (Messina-Firenze: D'Anna, 1971), p. 172.

29. F. C. Sainz de Robles, *Lope de Vega* (Madrid: Espasa, 1962), 203.

30. Góngora's letter is lost and its contents are known because we
possess Lope's reply to it. Góngora alludes to Lope's support
of a Helvidian heresy (one which denies the virgin birth, and
the one against which Saint Ildefonso wrote his treatise).

31. "Una nota lopiana y otra gongorina en una comedia del Fénix,"
Revista de filología española, 55 (1972), 314.

32. In "El papel de la nueva poesía," p. 197.

33. *Cronología de las comedias de Lope de Vega* (Madrid: Gredos,
1968), 296-298.

34. Specifically: "Al que más gallardamente pintare en un Soneto
la descensión de nuestra Señora a la santa yglesia de Toledo,
se dará un pomo de plata dorado: y el segundo una banda de
color con puntas de oro" (facs. ed., Valencia: A. Pérez Gó-
mez, 1951).

35. Although it was not printed until 1621, it was most probably composed, circulating in manuscript, already in 1617, according to Millé. See his "El papel de la nueva poesía," pp. 204, 206–212.

36. C. A. de La Barrera y Leirado, *Catálogo bibliográfico y biográfico del teatro español antiguo desde sus orígenes hasta mediados del siglo XVIII* (Madrid, 1860; rpt. Madrid: Gredos, 1969), pp. 173–174.

37. Lope de Vega Carpio, *El capellán de la Virgen,* ed. E. Juliá-Martínez, *Obras dramáticas escogidas*, I (Madrid: Hernando, 1934); also easy to use is the ed. of Marcelino Menéndez y Pelayo, vol. 30 of the Edición Nacional of his complete works (Madrid: CSIC, 1949). The play also appears, with notes by F. C. Sainz de Robles, in vol. 3 of Lope's *Obras escogidas* (Madrid: Aguilar, 1955).

AUTO DE LA
DESCENSIÓN DE
NUESTRA SEÑORA

AUTO FAMOSO DE LA DESÇENSION DE NUESTRA SEÑORA
EN LA SANTA YGLESIA DE TOLEDO, QUANDO TRUJO LA
CASULLA AL GLORIOSSISSIMO SAN ILEFONSO
SU SANTO ARÇOBISPO, Y PATRON NUESTRO [1]

COMPUESTO por mi señor y grande amigo, el Maestro Joseph de
Valdivieso, que haya gloria, y trasladado por mí el liçençiado
Francisco de Roxas para mayor honrra y gloria de Dios y de su
benditíssima Madre, virgen antes del parto, en el parto, y después del parto, y siempre virgen, virgen conçebida sin peccado
original, a pesar de los herejes traydores.

PERSONAS [2]

Nuestra Señora		Un Mudo Pobre
S. Leocadia	Florindo	Un Manco Pobre
S. Ilefonso	Braulio	Una Muger
Un Anjel	Pelagio	La Justiçia
El Rey	Una Vieja	Dos Alabarderos
Un Paje	Moscón	Un Capitán Niño
	Un Çiego Pobre	

PRIMERA ESCENA

(Salen dos herejes llamados Florindo y Braulio.)

Florindo: ¡Tiende tu lobuna capa,
              que es capa de pecadores, [3]
              pues eres del que haçe mal
              amiga, o amiga noche!

Pues te preçias , poco honesta,

con nieblas y sombras torpes,

de cómplice y de terçera

de torpeças y de amores,

piadosamente, si sabes,

las nieblas densas descoje,   10

con que vençiste en Egipto

del sol los rubios ardores. [4]

Entenebrezca tu rostro

estos fugitivos hombres;

así lamias[5]y hechiçeras

sangre te ofrezcan y flores,

ansí amadores incastos

y mudos escaladores [6]   f. 1v

de sus votos tus altares

temerosamente adornen.   20

Que de Teudio y de Pelagio

favorezcas los fautores,

que van de Toledo huyendo,

de David segunda torre, [7]

dese veçino del Çielo,

desa çiudad sobre monte,

desa escala de Jacob, [8]

dese milagro del orbe.

Dese Doctor nos defiende,

que con libros y sermones   30

nuestros trabaxados dogmas

ánjel confuta más que hombre;

del Moysés que con la vara

ondas encrespa feroçes, [9]

porque al gitano enemigo

dél conxeladas ahoguen;

del que nos echó del templo,

uno haçiendo como açote,

por que le haçemos (tal diçe)

espelunca[10] de ladrones;   40

del segundo Evangelista

que, rodeado de soles,

él *in prinçipio* escribió

de su virginidad noble;[11]

dese Ignaçio que en el pecho,

como el de Jesús su nombre,[12]

esculpe el de esa muger,

Reyna de los çielos onçe;

dese Ylefonso. . .

Braulio: Florindo,   50

ni le mientes, ni le nombres,

si no es que aumentar pretendes

dolores a mis dolores,

que es su nombre formidable   f. 2r

al obscuro Flejeronte[13]

como el de la que a Dios Niño

reclinó entre pajas pobres.

Florindo: ¿Qué haremos, Braulio, qué haremos?

Braulio: Que entre jarales y robles

a la Galia nos volvamos,   60

primero que nos lo estorbe

la pueriçia de Toledo.

Florindo: En armados esquadrones,

con piedras, palos, y espadas,

nos buscan puestos en orden.

Oye los pueriles cajas,   *(Tocan dentro.)*

los inquietos gritos oye.

Braulio: Debajo destos portales,

mientras que pasan, te absconde.

SEGUNDA ESCENA

(Salen los más niños que pudieren con espadas, plumas,[14] y

6

atambor, y Moscón, capigorrón,[15] armado a lo graçioso.)

Tamborilero:	Viva la virginidad	70
	de la çelestial María,	
	que antes del parto fue virgen,	
	en él, y después dél.	
Todos:	¡Viva!	
Tamborilero:	¡Muera Teudio con Pelajio,	
	con todos los de su seta,	
	y el hereje que no cre(e)	
	que madre quedó donçella!	
Todos:	(¡Mueran!)	
Niño Capitán:	¡Marche por todas las calles	80
	en orden la compañía,	
	y el bando que aquí se echó	
	en las plaças se repita!	
	Y qualqui(e)r blasfemo hereje	
	que con lengua desmentida	
	hablare mal del candor	
	de la que es más que el sol limpia,	f. 2v
	¡muera a pedradas y a palos!	
Moscón:	Videtur hec pena chica.	
Capitán:	Pues, ¿qué haremos?	90
Moscoñ:	Que imitetur	
	aut jigotum, aut salchicham.	
Capitán:	Gente pareçe que suena.	
Moscón:	Dato mihi linternillam.	

(Dásela y toma la linternilla a un niño.)
Heus tu, puer, et videamos
si est nobis gens inimica.

Capitán: Con las armas en las manos
todo el mundo se aperçiba,

y muera el que no dixere:
"Viva la Virgen María".   100

Todos: (¡Viva!)

TERCERA ESCENA

(Sale una vieja abrigada con una candelilla en la mano.)

Moscón: ¿Quis va, quis venid(sic), heus tu?

Capitán: ¿Pues agora latiniças?
            ¿Quién va allá?

Vieja: Una pobre vieja
            que ha diez años que maytina.

Capitán: Pues diga quién vive, madre.

Moscón: Yo la aconsejo que diga:
            "que la Virgen siempre virgen",
            aut probabit densas guijas.   110

Vieja: Vive la Madre de Dios,
            su pureça no ofendida,
            su eterna virginidad
            vive y viva siempre.

Todos: ¡Viva!

Vieja: ¿Qués esto, queridos hijos?

Capitañ: Es, madre, una compañía
            que en el nombre de tal reyna
            y su defensa milita.

Vieja: ¿Pueden reçibir mugeres?   120   f. 3r

Moscón: Reçipiatur, per mean vitan.

Capitán: ¿Mugeres? Es afrentarnos.

Moscón: Non, quia es quasi cofradía,
            audite rationen mean.
            Sed, ¿quare causa, o pueritia,
            iste exerçitus non marchat

8

ut hereticos occidad?
Non me miratur suspensus;
Di çito mihi si hay ira.
Pues, ¿quién mejor que esta cara   130
matabit mile heregías?
¿No buscan soldados viejos
para la buena miliçia?
¿Quién más vieja que esta vieja,
sin muelas y sin ençías?

Capitán;   Sepa que ha de pelear
con temeraria osadía.

Vieja: Por mi Virgen siempre virgen,
a mil quitaré las vidas.
Por vos, Virginidad Santa,   140
la espada es justo que ciña,
que Judic mató a Holofernes
y Jael al fuerte Sísara.[16]

Moscón: Expectate me poquitum.

Vieja: No es bien que hable algarabía.

Moscón: Sum catholicus christianus,
y aun sé toda la doctrina.
No ando por los çimenterios
con çercos ni candelillas,
ni me hallaron vuelto ganso,   150
volando de viga en viga.
Ante el señor Capitán,
dejando a salvo mi vida,
si eres hombre,¡sal aquí!

Vieja: ¿Tan presto se encoleriça?

Moscón: Madre, conozca a Moscón,   f. 3v
aguador de la familia
que fue del santo Arçobispo,

	y que agora se exerçita
	en servir al limosnero: 160
	llevaba las esportillas,[17]
	y es limosnero del brodio.[18]

Vieja: ¿Cómo, y el brodio le fían?

Tamborilero: Dos hombres, seor Capitán.

           (Empuñan las espadas y vense
               Florindo y Braulio.)

Capitán: Muriósenos la velilla.

Moscón: Digan quién vive, ea presto,
               o habrá crepitante china; [19]
               digan quién vive, ¿qué aguardan?

Florindo: Vive...

Moscón: Que tragan saliva.   170
               "La Virgen" digan, o sean
               de aqueste asador morçillas.

Capitán: ¿Quién vive?

Florindo: Vive la Virgen.

Capitán: Diga, ¿qué Virgen?

Florindo: María.

Capitán: Diga, ¿qué María?

Florindo: La Madre
               de Dios, virgen y parida.

Moscón: Pues digan luego que abjuran   180
               la depravada dotrina
               de Teudio y Pelagio, que ardan
               de alquitrán en llamas vivas.
               ¿Qué responden?

Florindo: Que abjuramos
               a todas sus heregías.

Moscón: ¡Digan que son unos cueros[20]

y que mienten! ¡Presto: digan!

Braulio: Deçimos que cueros son,

y quanto diçen, mentira.   190

Capitán: Pues recójanse, que es tarde.

Florindo: Que nos plaçe.   f. 4r

Braulio: Estraña dicha.

(Vanse los dos.)

Moscón: Pese a mi flema no hallara

de aquesta jente heretica[21]

siquiera media doçena

que desvalijar las tripas.

Capitán: ¡Marche a la Plaça Mayor

la devota Infantería,

y al son de las cajas todos   200

digamos: "La Virgen viva!"

Todos: ¡La Virgen viva!   *(Vanse.)*

CUARTA ESCENA

(Sale San Ylefonso con un libro en la mano.)

Ilefonso: Belleça del Sagrario, a vuestro bulto,[22]

por quien bienes el Çielo y graçias llueve,

como a mereçedor del sacro culto,

pues, como el vivo honestamente mueve,

este volumen, del ingenio inculto

parto el que pudo dar, si no el que debe,

de estilo pobre y de codiçias rico,

con toda el alma y coraçón dedico.   210

Infundid en el barro organiçado [23]

por mis débiles manos virtuosa

respiraçión y aliento derivado

de la vida del pecho generosa,

que con soplo vivífico informado,

elevada la parte ponderosa,

con tal virtud regida que a luz salga,

y lo que por mí pierde, por vos valga.

Del Sol de quien sois çentro, luz desçienda

que el sacrifiçio, que en el ara breve   220

la devoçión os sacrifica, ençienda;

y ençendido, gloriosamente eleve

su dicha en vuestras manos. Encomienda

leve paloma que en salir se atreve   f. 4v

del arca deste pecho discurriendo

tras la paz blanca por el mar tremendo.

Mirad, o Madre misericordiosa,

que vivís del hereje denostada,

que vos estáis de vos menesterosa,

que vos estáis de vos neçesitada: 230

a vos interçeded por vos piadosa,

y para vos con vos sed abogada;

a vos pedid por vos, Señora mía,

pues cuanto pide a Dios, puede María.

Ver que la mal cortada pluma mía

no escribió lo que debe me desvela,

y saber que escribió lo que podía

--no siendo de algún ánjel--me consuela.

Pues si el de la más alta xerarquía,

que más çerca del solio de Dios vuela,   240

lo escribiera mejor, que no lo dudo,

no lo que mereçéis, que nunca pudo.

QUINTA ESCENA
(Diçen dentro el Capitán de los niños y otros.)

Capitán:	¡Víctor, víctor, Ilefonso!
	¡Cola, Teudio con Pelagio![24]
Moscón:	¡Vítor, vítor, amus meus!
	¡Vítor, vítor, meus amus!

12

Capitán: ¡Vítor, la virginidad
del vientre siempre sellado!

Moscón: ¡Vítor, digo, aunque repese
a los hereges bellacos!   250

Todos: ¡Viva el pastor Ylefonso!

Moscón: Digo que viva, y bebamos.

Capitán: Aquí rotular podemos
al virginal abogado.

Moscón: ¿No atendéis que el sol flamenco,   f. 5r
con su rostro aborrachado,
sale por aquesos montes,
que matiça con sus rayos?

Ilefonso: Celebrad, hijos queridos,
el virginal desagravio   260
de quien fue en el parto virgen,
antes, y despúes del parto.
Cantad sonorosos versos
al montón de trigo casto,²⁵
a la Virgen siempre virgen,
arca y puerta, puerto y arco.²⁶
(Cantan dentro.)

Música: Los herejes lobos
huyen del pastor.
¡Mueran los vençidos!
¡Viva el vençedor!   (Çesa.) 270

Ilefonso: Cantad, hijos de la yglesia,
a la Madre del Amor
--entre espinas blanco lirio,²⁷
entre nubes rubio sol--
no a mí, que un flaco instrumento
de sus alabanças soy.
(Repite.)

13

Música:	¡Mueran los vençidos!	
	¡Viva el vençedor!	(Çesa.)
	(Sale Moscón.)	

Moscón: Yllustríssimo señor,
del Alcáçar ha salido   280
el Rey, del sol competido
de quien es competidor,
de grandes acompañado
y de mil títulos godos,
çircunferençia hechos todos   f. 5v
del Rey, que es su çentro amado.
Los clarines y trompetas
de que sale   dan señal
a las lenguas de metal,
hoy grandemente discretas;   290
avisan con dulçe son
las alegres chirimías,
dando nuevas de alegrías,
que sale la proçesión.

Ilefonso: Luego de vestir me den,
que no es bien que el Rey espere;
que honrrar la proçesión quiere,
honrrándome a mí tanbién.   (Vasse.)

Moscón: Hoy tarde se ha de yantar.
Quiero visitar las plaças   300
y manducarme en hogaças
(las que pudiere çampar),²⁸
una bota y un jamón;
porque comer a las tres
muy de caballeros es,
y es un pícaro Moscón.   (Vasse.)

SEXTA ESCENA

(Salen Florindo y Braulio, hereges, de peregrinos.)

Braulio:	¿De qué sirve que vistamos
	estos hábitos, me di?
Florindo:	¿De qué? Vestidos así
	hoy la proçesión veamos; 310
	que será mucho de ver,
	yendo en ella el Rey, advierte.
Braulio:	Más lo será nuestra muerte,
	si llegan a conoçer
	los muchachos a los dos.
Florindo:	No temas, Braulio; no harán,
	porque en la proçesión van f. 6r
	ocupados.
Braulio:	¡Plegue a Dios!
Florindo:	Goçaremos de las calles 320
	los adornos, las ventanas,
	y de tantas toledanas
	los rostros, picos, y talles.
	Yremos ansí a la vega
	hasta donde está enterrada,
	después de ser açotada,
	Leocadia, una moça çiega.[29]
	Goçaremos del buen día.
Braulio:	Hermoso para de invierno.
Florindo:	Que Amaltea[30] vierte el cuerno 330
	de sus flores, juraría.
Braulio:	El diçiembre me pareçe
	que se transforma en mil mayos,
	y que el sol con áureos rayos
	las nubes desapareçe.
Florindo:	Mezclémonos a la gente.

Entre tanta confusión
veremos la proçesión,
aunque escondidos.

Braulio: Detente,   340
repara en este aldeano.
¿Qué te pareçe?

Florindo: Ya entiendo.

(Sale Pelagio, herege, en hábito de labrador.)

Pelagio: De Toledo salgo huyendo
en este traje villano.
No así esclavo fugitivo
huyó, de temor helado;
no así pálido forçado
huyó, de cómitre esquivo;[31]
no así ladrón torpe huyó,   350   f. 6v
que del alguaçil se escapa,
casi asido de la capa,
en que çiego tropeçó;
como yo, entre asombro y miedo,
que deste disfraz me valgo
huyendo, y turbado salgo
dese peñón de Toledo.
¡Salva, o vestido, a Pelagio,
que muda vestido y habla!
Serás socorrida tabla   360
del que padeçe naufrajio.

Braulio: Digo que es él.

Florindo: Puede ser.

Pelagio: (Buen agüero, peregrinos.
(Aparte.)   Diréles dos desatinos,
pues no me han de conoçer.)

Florindo: A buen hombre, labrador,
hola, hermano.

Pelagio:	¿Qué pescuda? [32]
Florindo:	Que nos saquéis de una duda. 370
Pelagio:	Soy yo su desdudador.
Braulio:	¿Quién vive?
Pelagio:	Mi desventura, *(Conócelos.)*

mi dolor, mi pertinaçia
contra esa llena de graçia,
a mi pesar, Virgen pura.
Vive mi eterno dolor,
mi inmensurable tristeça,
de que sobre mi cabeça
triumfe su pie vençedor;   380
de que expelidos de España
salgan estos labradores,
que entre sus mieses y flores
sembraron letal çiçaña. [33]
Salgo huyendo a vela y remo   f. 7r
del que es en çiençia un abismo;
salgo huyendo de mí mismo,
que a mí contra mí me temo.

Florindo: ¿Qué esperas de aquesa suerte?
Pelagio, que si te ven,   390
es sin duda que te den
mil muertes en una muerte.

Pelagio: Escondido en una cueva [34]
un amigo me ha tenido,
hasta que en este vestido
última fortuna prueba.
Huyré entre escuros temores
dese invençible Toledo,
si no me detiene el miedo
que haçe las cosas mayores.   400
A la Galia volveré,

donde contra ese pastor
y el defendido candor
(1)íbelos[35] escribiré.
Contra la que ése sublima
escribiré con desvelo,
aunque es escupir al çielo
para que me cayga ençima.[36]
Escalaré el ayre puro,
y con impensado vuelo   410
pensad que he de haçer que el Çielo
no viva de mí seguro.
Turbaré sus luçes sumas,
y peleará mi deseo
contra manos de Briareo[37]
para escribir con çien plumas.

Florindo: Dentre el confuso tropel,
               sal a la gótica Galia.
               Deja a España, infesta[38] a Italia,   f. 7v
               más fáçil y menos fiel.   420

Pelagio: ¿Y vosotros?
Braulio: Partiremos
               dentro de dos o tres días,
               y los dogmas que porfías
               constantes defenderemos.

Pelagio: Mil abraços daros quiero.
               A Dios.
Braulio: El vaya contigo.

Pelagio: ¡Muera aquese mi enemigo
               como yo de envidia muero!   430   *(Vasse.)*

Florindo: Si te pareçe, atajemos
               las calles y al templo vamos,
               donde al Rey godo veamos.
Braulio: Sí, que es tarde, caminemos.   *(Vansse.)*

18

SEPTIMA ESCENA

*(Salen dos alabarderos, que se ponen a la puerta que no entre
gente, y hablan con la gente de adentro.)*

Soldado 1º: Entre por la otra puerta a la capilla,
que ésta no se ha de abrir de ningún modo,
hasta que llegue el Rey y el Arçobispo.

Soldado 2º: Pasen las religiones adelante,
y esperen con las cruçes y pendones;
tanbién puede pasar la clereçía,   440
que no podemos desdeçir del orden.

Soldado 1º: El Cabildo está aquí.

Soldado 2º: Pues entre y siéntese;
que sola la Çiudad y el Lugar tienen
para estas fiestas sus antiguos puestos.
Despojen, caballeros, que el Rey sale.
¡Plaça!

Soldado 1º: ¡Plaça, de aquí plaça, señores!

Soldado 2º: O por fuerça, o por grado, o por rigores.

*(Tocan chirimías y atabales. Salen el Rey Recesiundo
y San Ilefonso, con algunos caballeros que los acom-
pañan, y pónense de rrodillas en frente del   f. 8r
sepulcro de Santa Leocadia. Y Braulio y Florindo,
saliendo al paño, hablan con los soldados de guarda,
los alabarderos.)*

Braulio: Suplico a su merçed que dé liçençia   450
a estos dos peregrinos caballeros
para que, sin que ocupen, goçar puedan
de la çelebridad de fiesta tanta.

Soldado 1º: Entren, vuestras merçedes. Mas advierto
que al cabo se retiren de la yglesia.

Florindo: De buena gana. Y estimamos mucho
el favor y merçed que nos han hecho.

Soldado 2º: Que son más que pareçen, me sospecho.

Florindo:	Notable magestad el Rey sustenta.
Braulio:	Venerable persona el Arçobispo. 460·
	¡Si supiese quién somos!
Florindo:	Disimula.
Braulio:	Temblando estoy de miedo de miralle,
	que fuego tiene en ojos y palabras.
Florindo:	Calla, que cantan dulçes chançonetas
	con voçes repetidas.
Braulio:	Son discretas.
	(Cantan dentro.)
Música:	A Leocadia Ylefonso
	pide con ruegos,
	que la parte de tierra 470
	descubra el Çielo.³⁹ *(Çesa.)*
Rey:	Aquí en urna religiosa,
	a tanto thesoro breve,
	la porçión de grana y nieve
	en segura paz reposa.
	Descubre, Leocadia hermosa,
	a nuestro piadoso çelo,
	porque te honrre el patrio suelo,
	qué parte desta (se) ençierra⁴⁰ f. 8v
	el que fue çielo en la tierra 480
	y es tierra que ha de ser çielo.
Ylefonso:	Leocadia, honor de Toledo,
	que coronada de luz
	el alma diste a la Cruz,
	que esculpió el buril del dedo⁴¹
	al coraçón manso y ledo:
	que le alumbre, luz desçienda
	donde la sagrada prenda
	del cuerpo virgen habita,
	aunque por tal margarita, 490

hecho mercader, me venda.

(Cantan dentro, y sale Santa Leocadia cubierta con un velo de plata, una cruz en la mano derecha, y en la otra una palma.)

Música :

Ylefonso se alegre

con Leocadia bella,

pues que goça viva

la que buscó muerta. *(Túrbanse todos, y çesa.)*

Leocadia:

Por ti, o Ylefonso, vive

la Reyna nuestra Señora,

la Madre de Dios, María,

la que es madre y virgen sola.

Por ti la Estrella del Mar,   500

a quien encrespadas olas

escureçer pretendieron,

resplandeçe más hermosa.

A tu erudiçión y pluma

se constituye deudora,

y confiesa que te debe,

pues se la has dado, la honrra.

Por ti al soberano Rey

—una esençía en tres personas—

pareçe que le acreçientas,   510

siendo infinita la honrra.

Por ti la virginidad   f. 9r

que con permanente gloria

fue thálamo del Sol Dios

en la opinión vida cobra.

Yris de la Reyna vengo,

de luçes çeñida y rosas,

para anunçiarte la paz

en nube que el sol colora.

Como Michael armado,   520

o generoso Mendoça,

del Çielo de España expeles

al Dragón de negras conchas; [42]

Michael, "¡Quién como Dios?",

dixo en la suprema bola, [43]

y tú, "¡Quién como la Reyna",

dixiste, "Nuestra Señora?"

Los Serafines te ensalçan,

los Querubines te loan,

las Virtudes te bendiçen,   530

las Potestades te honoran;

las Dominaçiones cantan

tus alabanças heroycas,

los Prinçipados y Tronos,

tu resoluçión gloriosa;

los Arcánjeles, al son

de harpas, violines, tiorbas, [44]

a la Virgen siempre virgen

dan alegres la enbuenora;

los Anjeles, siempre gratos   540

al favor que a esta imperiosa

Emperatriz dar quisiste,

por ti mil justas convocan;

los Reyes y los Profetas,

padres de la casta Aurora,

componen en tu alabança

obras dignas de tus obras;

los Apóstoles, que han sido   f. 9v

de la fama de Dios trompas,

por las plaças de los Çielos   550

la tuya alegres pregonan;

los que en sangre del Cordero

tiñen las blancas estolas,

te aperçiben rojas palmas

y sus invictas coronas;

las Vírgenes de los lauros

con que sus frentes adornan,

estrellas entretejiendo,
guirnalda te haçen de gloria;
los Dotores de la Yglesia,   560
que beben néctar y ambrosia,
con sus plumas de oro escriben
tus virtudes generosas;
los penitentes del hiermo,
de sí mismos con vitoria,
en las murallas çelestes
tus banderas enarbolan;
los Inoçentes meninos,
todos con nupçiales ropas,
haçen danças, laços tejen,   570
cantando misas sonoras;
y en fin, ninguno en el Çielo
del Rey Trino el rostro goça,
que el parabién que les das
conmigo no le retorna.
Nuestra Señora la Reyna,
la que en todo exçede a todas,
sol de la virginidad
y de la belleça sola,
a visitarte me embía   580
de su parte, y ella propia
codiçia en venir a verte,
porque el coraçón la robas.
Espera mayor ventura,
y que entre flores y aromas,   f. 10r
luçeros, soles, y días,
pises çielos, goçes glorias.
Quédate a Dios, padre mío.

Ylefonso: Espera, blanca paloma,
después del vençido hereje   590
de la paz anunçiadora:
deja en tus nevados pies

que bese las breves formas,

y que el alma entre los labios

para adorarte se ponga.

Florindo: En caso tan admirable

las almas se vuelven locas.

Braulio: Mira a Ilefonso, que al Rey

el puñal turbado toma.

(Toma S. Ylefonso el puñal, o daga, al Rey y corta un pedaço del velo de la Santa.)

Mira que asido del velo,   600

que el virginal cuerpo adorna,

con respeto y devoçión

del velo una parte toma.

Mira que esparçiendo rayos

a su sepulcro se torna,

y que sobre el cuerpo hermoso

se vuelve la helada losa.

(Desapareçe la Santa con chirimías.)

Ilefonso: ¡Por la vida de Ilefonso,

que Leocadia mi Señora

está viva!

    610

Rey: Tus venturas,

O padre Ilefonso, goça.   *(Levántanse.)*

Ilefonso: El alma en los ojos tierna,

y el coraçón en la boca,

y en el Çielo boca y ojos,

mis dichas haré notorias.

Rey: Las flores apareçieron   f. 10v

a nuestra tierra dichosa,[45]

el sol bordando de luçes

sus nunca tocadas hojas.   620

La Tierra de Promisión

miel virgen y leche brota,[46]

y la Astrea soberana [47]

el Siglo Dorado torna;

el Aurora de María,

de sus lumbres precursora

vimos subir del disierto [48]

perlas vertiendo y aljófar.

Ilefonso: Oyóse en la tierra nuestra

la tortolilla amorosa, [49]   630

que regalando los ayres

çielos y tierra enamora.

Rey: Renaçió la phéniz bella

entre aromáticas gomas,

haçiendo la breve pira

juntamente cuna y fosa.

Ilefonso: ¡O velo, velo del Çielo,

por manos texido hermosas!

¡Qué sutil transparentaste

de marfil la virgen goda!   640

Velo del retablo hermoso,

que el Çielo es justo que asconda,

para que no le profanen

ojos que en la tierra lloran:

de la ymajen de Leocadia

fuiste cortina çelosa,

que tiene çelos el Rey

y a quien ama, estima y honrra.

Del çendal delgado hiçiste

viriles [50] a la custodia   650

que guarda un cuerpo de virgen

tan entero que me asombra.

Del sol de Leocadia bella   f. 11r

has sido nube piadosa,

porque no çegase el mundo

a sus radiantes antorchas.

Sol fue Leocadia, sol es;
y sol que al del çielo dora.
Y si se puso, ¿qué mucho
que nos dexase a su sombra?   660

Rey: El velo con el cuchillo
en el Sagrario se ponga
(si en fe de tan gran milagro
para perpetua memoria);
y en orden la proçesión
vuelva con la misma pompa,
dando a los Çielos las graçias
por tan admirables glorias.
        (Vanse y cantan.)

Música: Ylefonso se alegre
con Leocadia bella,   670
pues que goça viva
la que buscó muerta.   *(Çesa.)*

OCTAVA ESCENA

(Quedan los dos herejes.)

Florindo: Honrrosa resoluçión
causa en mí el caso presente.
Con su luz resplandeçiente
me ha alumbrado el coraçón.
Las palabras que por rosas
néctar y ambrosia esparçieron,
del arco del pecho fueron
flechas de luz poderosas;   680
la cruz que en su diestra vi
espada me pareçía
de fuego, y que la esgrimía
indignada contra mí;   f. 11v
la que mostró rubia palma

entre Çírculos de gloria,

la palma, triunfo, y vitoria

que consiguió de mi alma,

que de temor, entre el hielo,

que fuera, temió confusa,   690

la cabeça de Medusa,[51]

si corriera el sutil velo,

que con sus bellas facçiones

en piedra nos convirtiera.

Braulio: ¿Qué mucho quando lo hiçiera,

pues lo son los coraçones?

En tu pensamiento estoy:

Leocadia me ha convençido.

Como ciervo al agua herido,

a buscar mi salud voy.[52]   700

¡Qué alegre el alma atropella

los er(r)ores de Pelagio,

y espera en tanto naufragio

propiçia del Mar la Estrella!

Florindo: De mis errores me aparto,

confesando el alma mía

que antes virgen fue María,

en él, y después del parto.

Braulio: Alegre el alma confiesa

autoriçado el vellón,   710

la flor y fruto de Arón,

la çarça en el fuego ilesa.

Florindo: La puerta de Eççequiel,

la donçella de Ysaẏas,

la muger que Xeremías

vio çercar al varón fiel.[53]

Braulio: La que en graçia fénix una,

quedó donçella y parida,

del sol que vistió vestida,   f. 12r
y calçada de la luna. [54]   720

Florindo: A Ylefonso buscaremos,
               a quien llorosos los dos
               la hermosa Madre de Dios
               por virgen confesaremos.

Braulio: Los coraçones contritos
               amansarán sus enojos,
               diluvios vueltos los ojos
               que aneguen nuestros delitos.
               Pediremos que interçeda
               a la Virgen defendida   730
               pues, si le debe la vida,
               ¿qué habrá que no le conçeda?
               que nuestras culpas remita
               el Hijo, de su amor premio,
               y que de la Yglesia al gremio
               segunda vez nos admita.

Florindo: Que lo habemos de alcançar
               de su clemençia colixo,
               que lo deprendió del Hijo,
               que es muerto por perdonar.   740

Braulio: De entre çarças del error,
               del Lobo infernal heridas,
               estas ovejas perdidas
               vuelven a su buen Pastor.   *(Vansse.)*

NOVENA ESCENA
(Salen Moscón y un paje.)

Moscón: Vivit Dominus, Petre, que me pesa
               de que non vidi virginem Leocadiam
               ut diçis mihi, pulcram velut lunam
               y escoxidam ut solem.

Paje: Moscón mío,

¡si vieras levantar la inmóbil losa 750

por sí sola--si bien se presumía   f. 12v

que alguna esquadra de ánjeles hermosos

que acompañaron a Leocadia santa

con manos invisibles la levanta!

Pareçía que el Çielo distilaba

leche y miel en suspensos coraçones,

y que los coraçones levantados

en lágrimas alegres se exalaban

por los ojos que absortos la miraban.

Moscón: Di çito mihi, amiçe, si salibit 760

cun linteis del sepulcro, hoc est, mortaja;

que si salió de muerta, yo renunçio

por el miedo de ver (que soy medroso)

el gaudium del miraculo famoso.

Paje: Con un velo salió resplandesçiente,

luçes brillando de color de çielo,

con que a los çircunstantes deslumbraba

de modo que ninguno el rostro bello

vio de Leocadia virgen, sino sólo

el Arçobispo, mi señor, que pudo, 770

llamando:"¡Virgen de la Virgen pura!",

ver, por su gran virtud, tanta hermosura.

(Dentro diçe un pobre.)

Pobre: Deo graçias, padre Moscón.

Moscón: Ya los pobres han comido.

¡Den graçias, hermanos pobres,

y digan como yo digo:

"Viva la virginidad." *(Mira adentro.)*

Todos: Viva la virginidad.

Moscón: "Del intacto Paraýso."

Todos: Del intacto Paraýso. 780

Moscón: "Virgen Madre y Madre Virgen."

Todos: Virgen Madre y Madre Virgen.

Moscón:	"De Teudio a pesar y Elvidio."[55]	f. 13r
Todos:	De Teudio a pesar y Elvidio.	
Moscón:	Digan una "Ave María"	
	por mi amo el Arçobispo;	
	y en diçiéndola se vayan,	
	si quieren, con Jesuchristo.	
	Voy a repartir el brodio	
	a los hermanos mendigos, 790	
	con los pedaços de pan	
	y, de lo que sorbo, vino,	
	que me pareçe que suenan	
	sus voçes en mis oýdos	
	como abejas que susurran,	
	o como gruñen cochinos.	
	Quiero dar mi brodio en paz	
	más que el agua claro y limpio.	
	A maxis ver, patrón caro.	*(Vase.)*
Paje:	Moscón, Dios vaya contigo. 800	*(Vase.)*

DECIMA ESCENA

*(Salen pobres de diferentes figuras--un manco, un çiego,
un mudo, y otros dos o tres. Sale el çiego con un criado.)*

Çiego:	Quando saliere Moscón,
	avísame, mendruguillo,
	que si las coplas me estafa,
	las oraçiones le siso.
	Veme diçiendo por orden
	los que entran.
Criado:	El morteçino.
Çiego:	Es él que se finjió muerto,
	y diz que los llevó vivos.
Criado:	El mudillo. 810
Mudo:	Ba, ba, ba.

Çiego:	¿Para qué es "ba, ba" conmigo,	f. 13v
	seor mudo, si sé que charla	
	más que un hablante cautivo?	
Criado:	El mancante y el tullente.	
Çiego:	El que tulle y manca niños,	
	haçe llagas, y abre piernas.	
	Sor compadre, bienvenido.	
Manco:	¿Qué reçongla, [56] sor Palomo?	
	Como él, como de mi ofiçio;	820
	éste aprendí y éste exerço	
	con mil honrras,¡loor es Christo!	
	Tanbién, çiego de limosna,	
	manco y tullo a los amigos,	
	que alma tengo y soy christiano.	
Çiego:	Señores, es un bendito.	
Criado:	El tripero.	
Çiego:	El que el Alcalde	
	cojió con el artificio	
	de las tripas, y al pesqüeço	830
	con ellas le dio çien priscos.	
	(Sale una muger pobre.)	
Criado:	La gallinera.	
Çiego:	Ya entiendo	
	que las cría; que la digo:	
	es hoy briba [57] o vergonçona,	
	Mirarla quiero el vestido.	
Muger:	Miente, como çiego falso.	
Çiego:	¡Çiego falso, y desmentido!	
	Si eres hombre, sal aquí,	
	que a palos te desafío.	840
Manco:	No derramé yo el poleo, [58]	
	sor Palomo, o Palomino. [59]	

Çiego:	¿Rufianicos para mí?
	Señores, séanme testigos.
Mudo:	¿Qués esto, estando yo en vela?
	Dense las manos de amigos,
	que pareçemos bribones.
Çiego:	Su amigo soy, si lo es mío.
Manco:	En reçibiendo la sopa
	yremos ahogar en vino
	todos estos remoquetes.[60]
Çiego:	Etian, siendo bueno y frío.
Manco:	Entretanto, el sor Palomo,
	pues es poeta...
Çiego:	Desdigo.
	Abudiçe,[61] que no lo soy,
	ni lo he de ser, ni lo he sido.
	Yo soy çiego i muy honrrado,
	no poeta. ¡O qué lindico![62]
Mudo:	Pues, ¿es malo ser poeta?
Çiego:	Dios lo sabe, sor Desdicho.
Mudo:	¿No haçe coplas?
Çiego:	No, seor.
	Las que canto, otro las hiço.
Mudo:	Perdone.
Çiego:	Lindo es "Perdone",
	después de haberme ofendido.
Manco:	¿Hay alguna historia nueva,
	algún caso o milagrito?
Çiego:	Milagrito, y aun milagro,
	de los buenos que se han visto.
	¿No saben lo que pasó

f. 14r

850

860

870

... . Arçobispo

en la vega con la virgen
Leocadia? Es caso divino.
Ya se le di a componer
a un poeta de poquito,
que haçe coplas con ayuda.
La verdad es que es noviçio.
Seis quartos le di en señal   880   f. 14v
y quedéle a deber çinco.

Manco: Paso, que viene Moscón.   (Sale Moscón.)

Çiego: Seor Moscón, bienvenido.
            Mendrugo, dale la hortera.⁶³

Moscón: Hasta en el brodio hay peligro
            y desdichas.

Çiego: ¿Cómo es eso?

Moscón: Como el brodio se ha vertido.

Çiego: Es mal vertido, ¡por Dios!
            ¿Burlaráse el Mosconçito?   890

Moscón: No me burlo, hermano çiego,
            especialmente con pícaros.

Manco: Esa desgraçia, señor,
            por nosotros ha venido.

Çiego: No es christiano el que ansí agravia
            a todo aqueste pobrismo.

Muger: Verterse el brodio me güele⁶⁴
            a gula y a ladroniçio;
            mas podrá ser que lo allane
            mi señor el Arçobispo,   900
            que aunque llenos de remiendos,
            mancos, cojos, y tullidos,
            no le güelen mal los pobres,
            ni se le(s) çierra el oýdo.
                (Hablan aparte los pobres.)

Çiego:	¿No es mejor que a este Moscón,
	moscardo, mosca, o mosquito,
	con los palos hoy le demos
	la miel que dan los ençinos?
Moscón:	Vive Dios, que estoy temblando
(Aparte.)	más de miedo que de frío, 910
	que estoy solo y temer puedo
	de palos un torbellino.

f. 15r

(Çércanle a Moscón.)

	Colérico soy, mis pobres,
	perdonadme, pobres míos;
	que ya que no ha habido brodio,
	habrá cornado y bodigo.⁶⁵
Çiego:	Digo y hago.
Manco:	Doyle y voy.
Çiego:	Bodigo y cornado lindo,
	¿por barba? ⁶⁶ 920
Moscón:	Por barba pues.
Çiego:	¡O Moscón de Jesuchristo!
Moscón:	Esperen, que voy por ello.
Çiego:	¡Págueselo el Uno y Trino!
Moscoñ:	Por orden, todos, por orden. *(Vase Moscón.)*
Çiego:	Por orden y sin ruido,
	que es súpito el buen Moscón.
Manco:	Vaya a serlo a Peralvillo.⁶⁷
Mudo:	Para canónigo aprende.
Muger:	El aprende honrroso ofiçio. 930
Manco:	El Arçobispo, presumo,
	que viene con él.

(Sale San Ilefonso y Moscón.)

Ilefonso:	O hijos,
	mucho me alegráis el alma,
	que un Christo en cada uno miro.
	Llegad, abraçadme todos.
Moscón:	Timeas, oro te, pediculos.
Ilefonso:	No os retiréis. Abraçadme.
Çiego:	¡Ay, señor! No somos dignos.

Ilefonso:	Pegadme vuestros remiendos,	940
	que por çielos los cudiçio,	
	que disimuláis con ellos	
	divinamente a Dios mismo.	f. 15v
	Denles a cada uno un real	
	y un pan.	
Muger:	¡Viva treinta siglos	
	nuestro padre y padre santo!	

Çiego:	¡Santo, no más, y aun santíssimo!:	
	como del sepulcro vio	
	entre cánticos divinos	950
	salir la virgen Leocadia,	
	de rosas çercada y lirios.	
	Plegue a Dios que a honrralle venga,	
	que baje del çielo impíreo	
	María, Nuestra Señora,	
	que virgen ha defendido.	

Manco:	Dios le dé lo que mereçe.

Ilefonso:	Más me da que he mereçido.	
	Andad con Dios, y sed buenos.	
	Sed honestos y sufridos,	960
	que el coraçón me lleváis	
	entre los rotos vestidos.	

Moscón:	Pobre coraçón.
Ilefonso:	¿Por qué?

Moscón:	Porque morirá comido
	de piojos.
Ilefonso:	¡Calla ya, neçio!
	No me indignes, que me indigno
	como el buen amigo que oye
	hablar mal de sus amigos. 970
Moscón:	Muchos destos son mauleros⁶⁸

Moscón: Porque morirá comido
              de piojos.

Ilefonso: ¡Calla ya, neçio!
              No me indignes, que me indigno
              como el buen amigo que oye
              hablar mal de sus amigos.   970

Moscón: Muchos destos son mauleros [68]
              ed, magna ex parte, fingidos.

Ilefonso: Para mí son pobres todos,
              y a todos amo y estimo.
              No digas, Moscón, a nayde
              que con los pobres me has visto.

Moscón: Quando yo callar supiera,   f. 16r
              sus remiendos dieran gritos.
                        (Vanse los pobres.)

                    UNDECIMA ESCENA

        (Entran Braulio y Florindo, de peregrinos.)

Florindo: Deo graçias.
Ilefonso: Mira quién llama.   980
Moscón: ¿Quién llama?
Florindo: Dos peregrinos.
Moscón: Tarde vienen.
Ilefonso: Nunca es tarde
              para hacer lo que es debido.
              Abre y prevénles un baño,
              mesa, y camas sin gruñirlo,
              porque puede ser que vengan
              dos ánjeles de camino. [69]

Moscón: Si aquéstos ánjeles son,   990
              yo por querub me confirmo.

Braulio: Danos los pies, varón santo.

Ylefonso:	Los braços os aperçibo. *(Abráçalos.)*
	Muy en buen ora seáis
	a vuestra casa venidos.
	¿Qué queréis? ¿Qué pretendéis?
Florindo:	Mayor secreto pedimos.
Ilefonso:	Entremos, pues, acá dentro.

(Habla con Moscón.)

Aquesta noche maytino,[70]
que es víspera de la O;   1000
a los sacristanes dilo.
Y di que la hermosa ymajen
del Sagrario--a quien dedico,
con el alma que la adora,
de su defensión el libro--,
que sobre el altar mayor
la coloquen, advertidos
que de estrellas, sol, y luna   f. 16v
quisiera haçerla vestido.

Moscón:	Dicam, domine, al momento. 1010
Ilefonso:	Hermanos, vengan conmigo.
	Piensen que esta casa es suya,
	y yo más suyo que mío.
Florindo:	Quando el milagro que vi
	no me hubiera convertido,
	sin duda me convirtieran
	los que en Ylefonso miro. *(Vansse.)*
Moscón:	Plegue a Dios que no lo cojan
	donde sin verlo ni oýrlo
	estos hermanos romeros 1020
	me le dejen patifrío. *(Vasse.)*

DUODECIMA ESCENA

(Sale Pelagio con vaquero,[71] medio dormitando.)

Pelagio: ¡Tu cárçel quebranté fuerte,

lisonxero burlador!

¡O sueño despertador

de mi vida y de mi muerte!

Del lecho, con inquietas

ansias, huyo soñoliento

por potro de mi tormento,

donde hasta el alma me aprietas!

Y aunque con mayor crueldad 1030

de las que otras veçes sueles

me apretaste los cordeles,

no he de confesar verdad.

Si hablé mal desa muger,

ya lo dije, aunque se enoje

Dios y, enfadado, me arroje

al çentro del padeçer.

De su piedad desespero,

porque es tal mi obstinaçión f. 17r

que, aunque me ofrezca el perdón, 1040

ni le pido ni le quiero.

No sé si dispierto vi,

o soñando, que bajaba

la Justiçia, que vibraba

una lança contra mí;

que indignada me deçía,

castigada mi maldad:

"¡Viva la virginidad

de la çelestial María!"

*(Sale por lo alto la Justiçia, que es un Anjel,
con una lança que le pueda alcançar.)*

Mas, ¿qué es esto, ayrado Çielo? 1050

¿Contra mí tanto rigor?

A tu esquivo resplandor

me voy convirtiendo en hielo.

¿Qué me persigues? ¿Qué quieres,

de diamante armado y oro?

¿Por qué en vano a este Eliodoro[72]

turbas, persigues, y hieres?

(Diçe el Anjel como Ministro de Justiçia.)

Anjel: ¡Sal con destierro preçiso

entre abrojos y entre espinas,

ofensor de las divinas   1060

belleças del Paraýso!

(Tiembla Pelagio.)

De la yglesia es esta puerta

de mis desvelos guardada;

que es bien que la halle çerrada

el que la despreçió abierta.

¿Quántas veçes la que adora

el Çielo, de ti ofendida,   f. 17v

de tus culpas condolida,

fue clemente interçesora?

¿Quántas veçes, o villano,   1070

porque tu perdón codiçia,

la espada de la Justiçia

quitó al Hijo de la mano?

Como (a) Datán y Abirón,

¡se abra la tierra abarima,

donde con ellos oprima

tu rebelde obstinaçión![73]

Porque a la luz te atreviste,

entre sus rayos çegaste.

¡Cai en el laço que armaste![74]   1080

¡Cai en la cueva que hiçiste!

De las manos de la muerte,

darás en las del infierno,[75]

donde con dolor eterno

se alegre el Çielo de verte

Pelagio:	Pues ese infierno que espera,[76]
	que ardiendo no me reçibe.
Angel:	¡Quien como tú hereje vive,
	como tú es justo que muera!

(Dale con la lança y húndese Pelagio, y salen llamas de fuego, con ruido de cohetes.)

¡Baja entre gente traydora,   1090
opresa tu iniquidad!
¡Viva la virginidad
de la Reyna mi Señora!

(Dentro repite.)

Música :   ¡Viva la virginidad
de la Reyna mi Señora!   *(Çesa.)*

Anjel: ¡Y viva Ylefonso fiel,
defensor de su pureça,
a cuya docta cabeça   f. 18r
previene el casto laurel!
¡Viva Toledo, que adora   1100
con amor y piedad
la eterna virgin(id)ad
de la Reyna mi Señora!

(Repite.)

Música: La eterna virginidad
de la Reyna mi Señora.   *(Çesa.)*

Anjel: Eterno premio aperçiba
al que esta verdad venera.
El que la negare, ¡muera!,
y el que la creyere, ¡viva!

(Repite.)

Música: El que la negare, ¡muera!, 1110
y el que la creyere, ¡viva!   *(Çesa.)*

(Desapareçe la Justiçia.)

DECIMOTERCERA ESCENA

(Sale por abajo la vieja con un çamarro y una
linternilla, temblando de frío, que va a maytines.)

Vieja: ¡Con qué hielo se levantan

los benditos maytinantes,

a los coros semejantes

que maytines a Dios cantan!

Mas aunque caiga más hielo,

a mis maytines yré;

que estoy ya vieja y no sé

quándo daré quënta al Çielo.

Estaréme en un ri(n)cón;   1120

que es Dios tal que ser podría

que, más que el hielo me enfría,

me ençienda la devoçión.

Hiele bien, escarche harto,

que, aunque dé diente con diente,

tengo de hallarme presente

a la Expectaçión del Parto.   f. 18v

Y más, que Ylefonso santo

se hallará en ellos. Pues, ¿no?,

si la fiesta instituyó   1130

del misterio sacrosancto.

Diçen que más que la aurora

bella, en mudo regoçijo,

vio a Leocadia, que le dixo:

"Por ti vive mi Señora";

que con música del Çielo

la piedra se levantó,

y que humilde le cortó

parte del çelestial velo;

que suspenso en su luz bella,   1140

pedaços del alma llora;

y en mi alma pecadora

que me alegrara de vella.

Pero no me desconsuelo:

aquesta fe vive en mí,

que si entonçes no la vi,

espero verla en el Çielo.

(Esté hecho un altar, y en él una imajen de Nuestra Señora, de bulto, que parezca a la del Sagrario de Toledo, morena, la qual estará de forma que quando baje Nuestra Señora a dar la casulla al Santo, la pueda abraçar.)

¡Ay! La imajen del Sagrario

está en medio del altar.

¡O belleça singular!　　　　1150

Reçaréla mi rosario.

Morena, resplandeçéis

de mil hermosuras llena;

mas ¿qué mucho estéis morena,　　　f. 19r

si al Sol en braços tenéis?

El rosario reçaré.

¡Plegue a Dios que no me duerma!

Mas la vejez es enferma:

temo que me dormiré.

(Pónese a un lado con donayre y reça, y duérmese. Sale el Sacristán y Moscón a componer el altar y a ençender las velas.)

Moscón:　　Domine Sacristán, audite çimbala 1160

cum badaxis de hierro voçeando

ad clericos nocturnos que çelebren

las horas matutinas in honorem

de la que siempre fue pospartum virgo.

Sacristán:　　Dexe el latiniçar en estos tiempos.

Moscón:　　Omni tempore sum grande estudiante:

mi honor y mi latín va ya adelante.

Sacristán:　　Mire que es tarde; ençienda aquesas velas,

porque los maytinantes vendrán presto

y los devotos de la fiesta sacra,   1170

Expectaçión del Parto que intitulan,

en que las esperanças de la Virgen

de su divino parto se çelebran.

Moscón: Pues, ¿por qué de la O fiesta se nombra,

y la Yglesia con voçes disonantes

por estos ocho días la festeja?

Sacristán: Es fiesta de la O por la entereça

desta letra, a la eterna pareçida,

en que la Virgen nos parió la Vida;

tanbién porque la O nos representa   1180

las ansias, los deseos, las plegarias

de los padres del Limbo, deseando   f. 19v

ver a Dios Niño en un portal llorando.

Vieja: El sueño me ha vençido pereçoso.

Después le acabaré, señor rosario.

Perdóname, Morena de mi alma,

que soy muger y el sueño es porfiado.

(Duérmese.)

Moscón: Las velas ençendí. ¿Manda otra cosa?

Sacristán: Que registre los libros en el coro,

(y) prevenga las capas y los çetros,   1190

saque hisopo y naveta del sagrario,

y prevenga al inçienso el inçensario.

(Suena ruido como de truenos y tocan chirimías, y espántanse.)

¿Qué truenos y relámpagos son éstos

que ensordeçen y çiegan los sentidos?

¡En medio del invierno! ¡Gran portento!

Moscón: ¡Válgame el verbun caro, panem verum,

y la que veneratur Virgo virginum!

¡San Macario me valga y San Panunçio!

Casus aliquis novus tibi anunçio.

Sacristán:	Moscón, huyamos donde está la puerta. 1200
Moscón:	¡Paupérculo de mí, çiego he quedado!
Sacristán:	Estos son mis peccados, que son grandes.
Moscón:	Y como si lo son, digo los míos:

soy un bellaco y un marimaricas,

desdichado y fullero,[77] ¡miserere!

Siso el pan a los pobres, chupo el brodio,

meto el pan en la olla, soy poeta

y a más de treinta meses que lo uso.

Estas las culpas son de que me acuso.

Sacristán: Lléguese a mí.   1210

Moscoñ: Tras él me voy, adonde,

asido de su pie, vaya guiando.

Sacristán: Habemos de ir a gatas.   f. 20r

Moscón: Pues, ¿qué importa?

Sacristán: ¡Guarde los postes!

Moscón: Capud meum servabo.

Sacristán: ¡Música dulçe!

Moscón: Algún ladrón la espere,

como sonará bien al que se muere. *(Vanse los dos.)*

DECIMOCUARTA ESCENA

(Queda la vieja. Y descúbrese una nube y en ella Nuestra Señora, con una casulla en las manos, çercada de ánjeles, y Santa Leocadia. Tocan chirimías y canta la Música.)

Música: A vestir a Ylefonso   1220

viene María

casulla de estrellas,

soles, y días.   *(Çesa.)*

N. Señora: Cantad, O músicos míos,

a mi regalado amante,

mientras que yo a medianoche

rondo su puerta y su calle.

Del Çielo bajo por él;
deçilde que se levante,
pues, tras que verle, deseo   1230
un vestido que traygo darle.[78]
Edades juzgo las horas,
siglos juzgo los instantes;
porque a dos que bien se quieren
siempre para verse es tarde.
De que a estas horas le busco,
de mí todo el mundo hable;
aunque si a los dos conoçe,
¿en qué podrá mormurarse?
Abre, Ylefonso Pastor,   1240
abre y hallarás, si abres,
que sin çelos de mi Esposo,   f. 20v
he venido a visitarte.
Yo, fiadora, si supieras,
Dotor, que andaba a buscarte,
que hecho braços, que hecho ojos,
tú salieras a buscarme.
Al Hijo que parí virgen
--que soy donçella y soy madre--
vestí de tierra; y de Çielo   1250
bajo a vestirte y a honrrarte.
A él del Çielo le truje
para vestirle de carne;
y a mí a vestirte de Çielo
hasta tu casa me traes.
Para que yo le vistiera,
me rogó con un arcánjel;
y yo con este vestido
vengo con mil a rogarte.
Ymitas al Padre Eterno,   1260
que si me dio vida y Padre,[79]
tú la del honor me diste,

que en el honor me adoraste.

Ymitas al Hijo Eterno,

pues si él redimió a su Madre,

tú redimiste mi honor

de unos piratas alarbes.[80]

Ymitas al Amor Neugma,

que vino a mí en forma de ave;

sombra a mi pureça haçiendo   1270

con tus plumas elegantes.

Capitán de mi Limpieça,

así es justo que te llame:

como dixo Xeremías,

"ven a verme y a alegrarme."[81]

Ven, apóstol en la fe,   f. 21r

ven, en las vitorias mártir,

evangelista en la pluma,

en la lengua, dotor grave;

ven, virgen en la pureça,   1280

ven, en las venturas ánjel,

en la çiençia querubín,

serafín en tu amor grande.

Ven, y vengas en buen hora,

de mi amor christiano Adlante,[82]

que has alegrado mis ojos,

como el alma me robaste.

(Sale San Ylefonso y túrbase.)

Ilefonso: ¡Ave María! ¿Qué es esto?

¿Qué voçes oygo süaves?[83]

¿Qué Çielos por estos postes? 1290

¿Qué soles por estos ayres?

Fugitivos con los[84] hachas,

me desamparan los pajes,

y turbados y amarillos

encuentro los sacristanes.

¡Animo, coraçón mío!,

que no hay amador cobarde;

que si Dios es con nosotros,

no nos puede ofender nayde.

¿Qué es esto? ¡Gran visión!   1300

Bien será que me descalçe,

como a la çarça Moysés

entre las llamas constantes.[85]

Pareçe un carro de fuego,

que del Çielo al suelo baje,

si no Elías,[86] la hermosura   f. 21v

que es a Dios más semejante.

Pareçe que entre humo y nieblas,

aunque sin los animales,[87]

miro el Çielo, si no lleno   1310

de Dios, lleno de su Madre.

A la falda me pareçe,

que del árbol fulgurante,

el sol vestido de nieve

çiega en las luçes que esparçe.

¿Podré deçir, como Esteban,[88]

mi rostro no como un ánjel,

que los Çielos miro abiertos,

y en ellos la Virgen Ave?

N. Señora: Ylefonso.   1320

Ilefonso: ¡Dulçe voz!

Suenen tus açentos graves

al alma por el oÿdo,

que dentro de sí no cabe.

(Híncase de rrodillas a sus pies.)

Arrojaréme a esos pies

de jazmines y de aça(ha)res.

¡Intacta virginidad!

¡Madre de Dios, Virgen Madre!

(Reparte un ánjel las velas.)

Vieja:	¿Duermo o velo, coraçón?
	Si es que estáis en mí, avisadme: 1330
	si duermo, los Çielos veo;
	si velo, venturas grandes.
	¿No es ánjel el que las velas
	con faz risueña reparte?
	Señor ánjel, no me olvide.
	Déme vela.
Anjel:	Que me plaçe;
	tome, mas con condiçión
	que ha de volvérmela, madre. f. 22r
Vieja:	Démela una por una. 1340
Anjel:	¿Volverála?
Vieja:	Dios lo sabe.
N. Señora:	Llega, siervo fiel, llega y reçibe [89]
	este don de los Çielos de mi mano,
	mientras que subes al que te aperçibe
	de esençial gloria el Terno Soberano.
	Por ti, Dotor egregio, mi honor vive,
	y vivirá, a pesar de Elvidiano, [90]
	çercado de laureles y de palmas,
	en libros, templos, coraçones, y almas. 1350

    (Échale la casulla.)

Reçibe en prenda de la eterna paga
ésta, de voluntad, para que entiendas
que al Hijo amante que mis deudas paga
ni le duele la paga ni las prendas.[91]
Espera que a tus obras satisfaga
con la mejor de todas encomiendas,
de que conmigo el hábito te embía
de Maestre, sirviéndote María. [92]
Y porque más tu dicha se çelebre,
a Dios busque, Ylefonso valeroso,   1360

entre animales rústico pesebre,

y a ti, entre ánjeles mil templo famoso.

Quando el vital estambre Atropos quiebre,

que en el huso está hilando presuroso

de su tarea, Clotos[93] desabrida,

conmigo subirás a mejor vida. [94]

(Cantan y vístele la casulla.)

Música: ¡O qué bien os está el vestido

que la Reyna del Çielo os da!

Nadie dirá que no os viene naçido:

¡O qué bien, O qué bien que os está! *(Çesa.)* 1370

Ilefonso: Alma Virginidad, ya que no tenga   f. 22v

de puro serafín los labios de oro

en saber alabar quanto convenga

ni thesorera tal ni tal thesoro,

rudo diré: ¿De dónde a mí que venga

la hermosa Madre del Señor que adoro,

si bien no con el Sol en las entrañas

mas hecha un sol del Tajo a las montañas?[95]

¿De dónde a mí que, no en el tiempo estivo,

como al esperançado Patriarca,   1380

que hospedó cortésmente y conpasivo

los tres con parca mesa y fe no parca,[96]

pero çercado de splendor nativo

de la que es de amor arco y de Dios arca,

mejor que Obededon el arca hospedo,

con goço de David, de Oza con miedo?[97]

Diré, Beldad que querubines pisa,

que quedará presente en la memoria

del clero toledano por divisa

y eternas armas la presente historia; 1390

y diré que, antes de enpeçar la misa,

me cantaron los ánjeles la Gloria,

y que tras ella, con favor notorio,

me quisistis haçer el Ofertorio.[98]

Alabarme podré que desçendistes

donde a desora, Virgen, me esperastes,

y que en secreto me favoreçistes,

y de amor vuestro prendas me dejastes;

y que deçir a todo el mundo distes,

que os conoçió en lo hermoso que bajastes,   1400

y que las piedras lo dirán, que osaron

ser Çielo de las plantas que besaron.[99]

En esta piedra donde asiento toma,

vuestra presençia hermosa hará su nido,   f. 23r

del rigor acosada la paloma

donde hallará clemente al ofendido,

que es piedra que, después de la de Roma,

al eriço entre picas escondido[100]

servirá de refugio, donde pueda

huir de Dios la indignaçión azeda.[101]   1410

*(Nuestra Señora se vuelve al altar y abraça a
la santa imajen que está allí.)*

N. Señora: Antes que al Çielo vuelva, O imajen mía

yllustre del Sagrario, he de abraçarte

y, del santo esplendor del que me imbía

comunicando, mil belleças darte.

La gloria que me baña de alegría

quisiera, alma beldad, comunicarte;

mis dichas y mis bienes repartirte,

vida alentarte, espíritu infundirte.[102]

Como una a ti y a mí nos considera,

a ti y a mí un mismo culto ofreçe,   1420

por ti a mí me engrandeçe y me venera,

por ti a mí me honora y engrandeçe,

de mí por ti la interçesión espera,

a ti por mí alcançada la agradeçe.

Por ti en el Çielo me conozco honrrada,

y tú por mí en la tierra venerada.[103]

(Vuelve a abraçar la umajen.)

Adios, Anjel de Guarda de Toledo

y Reyna de los Anjeles; contigo,

aunque al Çielo me voy, copiada quedo,

y trasformada en mí, subes conmigo.   1430

    (Chirimías.)

Padre Ylefonso, adiós.   *(Desapareçe.)*

Ilefonso: Mal sin vos puedo   f. 23v

vivir, que ansioso y desalado os sigo;[104]

y aunque con palio de mejor Elías,

voçes daré a la gloria de las mías.[105]

Anjel: Madre, déme la vela.

Vieja: Anjel bendito,

perdone su merçed.

Anjel: ¿De aquesa suerte

la vuelve? ¿Y si por fuerça se la quito?   1440

Vieja: No hará, porque sabré haçerme fuerte.

Anjel: ¡Gran devoçión!

Vieja: Guardarla soliçito

para el tránsito triste de la muerte.

¡No me la quite!

Anjel: Guárdela en buen hora.

Vieja: ¡Viva, viva la Reyna mi Señora!

Ilefonso: Después de averos visto, ¿qué me queda

en la tierra que ver, O beldad alma?

Hasta volver a veros, ¿con qué pueda   1450

los ojos consolar, quietar el alma?

Dexar de veros el favor azeda

de averos visto. Se alboroça el a(l)ma,

porque al que os vio, si sabe conoçeros,

es la pena mayor dejar de veros.[106]

¿Qué graçias, Todahermosa, podré daros,

si el favor de la vuestra no me viene?

O ¿con qué voz intentaré alabaros,

quando Dios tanto que alabaros tiene?

¿Qué cánticos yrán a acompañaros,   1460

y a ymitaçión del que escucháis perene,

en dulçe açento de sus mentes puras?,

que al sol, que va tras vos, dexáis ascuras.

Como del monte a la sagrada falda,   f. 24r

que en sierpes de christal i en blanda risa

ofreçe en canastillos de esmeralda

flores la fuente, (c)uya marjen pisa,

mira bajar con la febea guirnalda

la jente que le espera çircunçisa

a la voz de Faraón, de Dios privança,[107] 1470

que todo quanto quiere dél alcança:

ansí pareçe que de aliento ajenos

a la puerta del templo, conturbados

entre nubes, relámpagos, y truenos,

tengo de hallar los tímidos criados;

pues que con rayos de hermosura llenos,

de la Madre del Sol comunicados,

bajo del monte donde vi su gloria,

dando fin dulçe a la sabrosa historia.[108]

FIN

En 21 de março, sábado, çerca de la una del mediodía,
año de 1643 años, día del glorioso San Benito, le acabé
de trasladar.

NOTES TO THE TEXT

Abbreviations used:

Correas   Gonzalo Correas. *Vocabulario de refranes y frases proverbiales.*

.Covarr.   Sebastián de Covarrubias. *Tesoro de la lengua castellana o española.*

Dicc. Aut.   *Diccionario de Autoridades, I-III.*

DRAE   *Diccionario de la Real Academia Española*, 1970.

* * * * * * *

1. The Lanini copy is titled: "Auto de Nuestra Señora y del glorioso St. Ylefonso".

2. This list, in the Lanini copy, omits the *muger* and the *dos alabarderos*; the *çiego, mudo,* and *manco* are called *tres pobres*, and Moscón's name appears with the sobriquet *capigorrón*.

3. The line has proverbial status; see Correas, 185a: "La noche es kapa de pekadores."

4. Exodus 10:21-23, the ninth of the ten plagues visited upon the Egyptians. Florindo is only partly right in his recall, for only the Egyptians were plunged into darkness: *ubicumque autem habitabant filii Israël, lux erat.*

5. *Dicc. Aut.* II, 354, says the ancients were divided over what *lamias* were. They were certainly evil, female (perhaps half serpent), and occasionally carnivorous. For Valdivielso, it surely refers to "una muger hechicera que se comía o chupaba los niños, lo que corresponde oy à nuestras bruxas." In which case, he is indulging in line 15 in a little synonymy.

6. *Escaladores* are cat burglars who work their crimes under cover of darkness (see *Dicc. Aut.* II, 549).

7. *"Sicut turris David"*: Canticles 4:4 " . . . que sirve de atalaya para descubrir los enemigos si vienen, y para mostrar el camino a los que pasan: todo lo cual conviene perfectamente a los prelados, pastores y doctores de la Iglesia, que deben estar siempre en vela para defensa de la piedad y de la fe" (*La Santa Biblia*, 3 [Madrid: Gaspa y Roig, 1852], p. 418).

8. Genesis 28:11-19. Toledo's importance as a door to Heaven is stressed in the comparison. Jacob told his questioners that his dream ladder was not earthly: *Non est hic aliud, nisi domus Dei, et porta caeli* (v. 17).

9. Exodus 14 narrates the parting of the Red Sea. Moses is here a figure of Ildefonso, his rod is Ildefonso's *De virginitate*, the believers are the faithful who pass through dry, and the heretic doubters of Mary's virginity the drowned pursuers.

10. *Espelunca.* This is a lair, a den, a hiding place (*Dicc. Aut.*, II, 599): it is part of the "lobuna" image pattern which began this discourse (see also 1. 1087).

11. John 1:1. Like the Evangelist John, who penetrated the mystery of Christ's being *in principio*, so has Ildefonso imparted wisdom about Mary's virginity *in prinçipio* in his writings.

12. Ildefonso lived seven centuries before Ignatius of Loyola (1491-1556), founder of the Jesuits. The comparison of Ildefonso, in 1616, to Ignatius (beatified in 1609, canonized in 1622), however, would work to magnify Ildefonso's reputation.

13. A tributary of the Acheron and into whose sulphurous waters were cast the souls of criminals. The name of Ildefonso is—like Mary's—feared in Hell.

14. In cant, *pluma* referred to an oar or a paddle, and this seems to be its meaning here, especially if we can equate the "espadas, plumas" here with the "palos y espadas" of 1. 64. The similarity of shapes might account for the semantic shift involved. See *Dicc. Aut.*, III, 302.

15. According to *Dicc. Aut.*, I, 143, the adjective describes the dress of those, especially students, who lead licentious lives.

16. There is humor in the old woman's comparison of her zeal in the pursuit of Mary's honor to the bloody deeds of her biblical predecessors. For Judith and Holofernes, see Judith, chaps. 8-16; for Jael and Sisara, see Judges, chaps. 4 and 5.

17. *Esportillas* are woven reed carriers (*Dicc. Aut.*, II, 612), in which, as *aguador*, Moscón transported his water jugs.

18. *Brodio.* "El caldo con algunos trozos de legumbres y sobras de la olla, que de ordinario se da à los pobres . . . ." (*Dicc. Aut.*, I, 687).

19. The threat of stoning (see also 11. 88, 110) is perceived here with humor, either as a rain of stones ("chinas") or—more metaphoric and onomatopoeic—the sound of cracking skulls.

20. *Cueros.* "Por traslación festiva se llama assi al borracho o gran bebedor" (*Dicc. Aut.*, I, 686). From the wineskins or "cueros", the meaning shifts to the tipplers, who, while under its spell, boast extravagantly with little regard for truth.

21. The meter and rhyme pattern show that the adjective here is paroxytonic.

22. The forty lines extending from 203-242 are five *octavas* of his own which Valdivielso has borrowed from *Sagrario de Toledo*, Book 12 (on 203v, 204r, 204v, 207v, and 208r). There are small variants in all of them, the most important occurring in the opening line, where the opening narrative statement, "Virgen, el santo dize a vuestro bulto", is now Ildefonso's direct appeal, "Belleça del Sagrario, a vuestro bulto."

23. *Barro*. The humble opening prayer is a topos of course, if here a specially vivid one in which Mary is being asked to breathe life and meaning into the clay of Ildefonso's desire to mold arguments in defense of her virginity. Other correlatives of the topos also appear: the feelings of insufficiency (235-236) and the consolation of having made an honest attempt (237-238).

24. *Cola*. "Entre los antiguos estudiantes, voz de oprobio, en contraposición de la aclamación o vítor" (DRAE, p. 319, no. 9).

25. Canticles 7:2 "Venter tuus sicut acervus tritici, vallatus liliis."

26. A common conceit (it is used again, in part, at l. 1384) which Valdivielso employed also in *Sagrario de Toledo*, Book I, on 13r: "Yo Palma, Nardo . . . / Arco, y Arca, Paloma, Puerto, y Puerta." Also from Canticles.

27. Canticles 2:2 reads: "Sicut lilium inter spinas, sic amica mea inter filias."

28. Valdivielso is careful to see that Moscón's language reflect his picaresque nature; thus "manducar" for comer (at l. 301; see *Dicc. Aut.*, II, 476) and, here, "çampar", which "vale también comer con apresuración descompuesta y excesivamente" (*Dicc. Aut.*, III, 553).

29. Leocadia was martyred in the time of Dacian (304 A. D.) for not abjuring her faith. She is a Patron Saint of Toledo. Her blindness seems part of a later version of her martydom.

30. Amaltea was a famed Cretan who sustained Jupiter for a period on goat's milk. She became then part of a constellation formed of a goat and two kids; the goat's horns--it was said--would pour out ambrosia and nectar when tilted (Covarr., 109).

31. *Cómitre*. The official put in charge of galley slaves (cf. the "forçado" of l. 348) and of meting out their punishments. The saint-heretic context enriches its connotations.

32. *Pescuda*. It is the equivalent of "preguntar" but may point to humble origins for Pelagio, since "oy tiene uso entre la gente rústica" (*Dicc. Aut.*, III, 242).

33. *Çiçana*. Discord, dissension, a pernicious custom introduced where only good practices hold sway (see *Dicc. Aut.*, III,

568). Valdivielso's biblical source is Matthew 13: 24-30.

34. The "cueva" echoes the reference at 1. 40 to "espelunca de ladrones" and develops further the *lobuna* pattern, used extensively throughout the auto (see 1. 1).

35. The Roxas copy reads "Ni velos", which makes little sense. I
have given the reading from the Lanini copy. Pelagio is here
shown to be smug and proud, literally condemning himself in
declaring that he will set out to write "libelos".

36. Pelagio senses that his efforts will be in vain. For interesting readings of the refrain, "escupir al viento", see
Covarr., p. 545, and Correas, 148b and 629b.

37. Briareius, a giant, son of Ge and Uranus. He had fifty heads
and a hundred arms and used them all for evil. Even though
Pelagio had a hundred pens in each of his Briareius-like
arms, he would still be fighting an uphill battle.

38. *Infesta* in the Roxas copy; the Lanini copy reads: *infecta* (fr.
"inficionar"), to foul the air with evil odors (see Covarr.,
p. 736). *Dicc. Aut.*, II, 264, tells us that *infestar* often
overlapped the meanings of *inficionar*, and so I have retained
the Roxas copy's reading.

39. Although the gathering takes place at the "sepulcro de Santa
Leocadia", the exact location of the physical remains of the
martyr were, and had long been, unknown. See also the allusion
in 11. 476-81, below.

40. Lanini's copy has the "se" which is crossed out in Roxas' copy.
Both, however, give "desta" which must agree with, anticipating
it, the "tierra" which follows, and not "deste"--to agree with
the preceding "patrio suelo".

41. In awaiting her certain death, Leocadia had so often made the
sign of the cross with her finger on the stone of her cell
wall that a permanent impression was made. She will appear
later holding a cross, her iconographical attribute. For its
dramatic effect, see 11. 681-683.

42. The Apocalypse of Saint John, chap. 12, verses 7ff., tell how
the Archangel Michael led his band of angelic warriors to vic-
tory over Satan, called *dragón*. The "negras conchas" are the
dragon's (i. e., Satan's) scales (Cf. Covarr., p. 346: "la cubierta dura de algunos pescados"). Lanini's reading at this
point, "de negra cola", is less dramatic, less vivid.

43. *Suprema bola*. The highest sphere (*Dicc. Aut.*, I, 637).

44. *Tiorbas*. "Instrumento Músico, especie de laud, algo mayor, y
con más cuerdas" (*Dicc. Aut.*, III, 279).

45. Lines 617-618. Almost a literal translation of Canticles 2:12:
"flores apparuerunt in terra nostra".

46. *Miel y leche.* Symbols of abundance associated with the Promised Land in Exodus, Leviticus, Numbers, Deuteronomy, and Joshua, *passim.* The biblical order is almost always, however, *lacte et melle.*

47. *Astrea.* Yet another image suggestive of plenty and perfection. In Greek mythology, Astrea was daughter to Zeus and Themis, and a symbol of Justice (not depicted with blindfolds, but instead a balance scale). When the Iron Age threatened the Golden Age with extinction, Astrea was the last of her kind, according to Ovid, to return to the safety of the heavens. The constellation Virgo also represents Astrea. In the text, her name—associated with Leocadia's—is herald of a new Golden Age, along with other "precursor" images in the series extending from 1. 617 to 1. 628.

48. The image is taken from Canticles 3:6; see also 8:5.

49. An almost literal translation of Canticles 2:12: "Vox turturis audita est in terra nostra".

50. *Viriles.* These were small glass pieces fitted on reliquaries to permit viewing of the relics within (see Covarr., p. 1006).

51. The eyes of Medusa, which could turn a person to stone, turn up in an unusual context: compared to the eyes of a saint. The effect Valdivielso achieves dramatizes the didactic import of the passage: The same "radiantes antorchas" (1. 656) will seem to fall sweetly on believers (Ildefonso) but be deadly to non-believers (Florindo, Braulio).

52. Compare Psalms 41:1: "Quemadmodum desiderat cervus ad fontes aquarum: ita desiderat anima mea ad te, Deus".

53. Lines 710-716 are a series of Old Testament prefigurations of the Virgin Birth: for Gideon's fleece, Judges 6:37-38; for Aaron's flowering rod, Numbers 17: 1-8; for Moses' burning bush, Exodus 3:2; for the eastern door of the temple, Ezekiel 44:2; for the virgin who would bear fruit, Isaiah 7:14; and for the passage concerning the woman who would seek out a man, Jeremiah 31:22. A similar series, on which this one is clearly modeled, appears in *Sagrario de Toledo,* Bk. 7, 124v-127r.

54. For the image, see the book of the Apocalypse of Saint John, 12:1-2.

55. This Elvidio has not been mentioned until now. He is a fourth-century Arrian heretic whose denial of the virgin birth—and other unusual ideas—were denounced at the Council of Capua in 391. St. Jerome had dealt effectively with this heresy in *Adversus Helvidium* (and this may have inspired Ildefonso's *De virginitate*; Ildefonso had written his own *De viris illustribus* after similar works by Jerome, Gennadius, and Isidore).

56. *Reçongla.* Modern "rezonga" (with the noun, "rezonglón, -ona") an onomatapoeic word suggestive of grumbling or complaining.

57. *Briba*. One who lives by *bribia*, the picaresque art of feign-
    ing misery (*Dicc. Aut.*, I, 681). See also Correas, p. 194a
    ("bivir del sudor axeno") and 607b. See also 1. 847, "bri-
    bones".

58. *Poleo*. A strong-smelling herb (Covarr., p. 875) known to be
    effective in killing fleas. However "derramar poleo" had a
    proverbial meaning as well: "Dízese de los ke hablan kon ale-
    gría y plazer, y jatan de huelgas, i dizen kosas gloriosas"
    (Correas, p. 689a). In the context, I take it to mean some-
    thing like "I didn't start this banter (but you did)". See
    the next note for further jocose meanings possible here.

59. *Palomo, Palomino*. In the exchange of insults, "palómo" is
    cant and the equivalent of "necio, simple" (*Dicc. Aut.*, III,
    98). While it also is the male dove or pigeon, and "palo-
    mino" is its fledgling offspring, this latter also alluded
    to a small fecal stain on an undergarment. The strong smell
    of the "poleo" in the previous line does suggest that the
    present banter centers on odors, jesting that would not be
    to the liking of the blind man, who normally has the upper
    hand in these exchanges.

60. *Remoquetes*. Verbal barbs, insults. See *Dicc. Aut.*, III, 569.

61. *Abudiçe*. This is the MS reading, which I have been unable to
    resolve or interpret satisfactorily.

62. Spoken ironically. Of proverbial nature (Correas, 166a).

63. *Hortera*. A wooden bowl, often seen on the belts of the poor,
    ready for receiving charitable offerings of food.

64. *Güele*. For "huele"; see also line 903. This is the only use
    of this pronunciation in the *Descensión*.

65. *Cornado y bodigo*. The first is a small coin (Covarr., p. 358;
    Dicc. Aut., I, 597) and the second an individual loaf of a
    wheat flour bread, normally used as an offering at weddings
    (*bodas*, whence its name, *Dicc. Aut.*, I, 635). For Ildefonso's
    approval of such an expenditure, see 11. 944-945.

66. *Por barba*. A pro-rata distribution of something (see Covarr.,
    p. 193).

67. Another sample of the sharp wit of the *manco*. In Peralvillo,
    near Ciudad Real, summary justice had become legendary. "La
    justicia de Peralvillo: que después de asaetado el hombre le
    fulminan el processo" (Covarr., p. 862). See also Correas at
    91a, 134a, and 186-187 (incl. n. 17).

68. *Maullero*. "Se toma también por embustero y engañador, con
    artificio y dissimulado" (*Dicc. Aut.*, II, 516).

69. The two Angels welcomed as travellers by Lot and his wife who
    led them from the city before its destruction (Genesis 19).

58

70. That is, Ildefonso will celebrate màtins (midnight) for the feast of the Expectation of the Virgin Birth. The date of the feast is December 18, and it is described somewhat at lines 1174-1183, below.

71. *Vaquero.* A "sayo de faldas largas" (Covarr., p. 993).

72. *Eliodoro.* The most logical Heliodorus here is a minister to Seleuco IV (187-175 B. C.), King of Antioch. On an inspection tour, Heliodorus attempted to lay hands on the treasure of the temple in Jerusalem when, suddenly, he was struck down by one Angel and severely beaten by two others. That he attempted such desecration against advice to the contrary and was struck down by an avenging Angel are obvious parallels exploited here with the presentation of the unrepentant Pelagio.

73. Lines 1074-1077. Datán and Abirón were two who conspired against Moses and Aaron and were punished by being swallowed by the earth. "Tierra abarima": Abarim is the area of high terrain to the east of the Dead Sea from where, it is said, Moses first gazed down upon the Promised Land.

74. *Armar lazo.* "Buscar ocasión y darla como otro cayga en trabajo"; *caer en el lazo:* "estar en el trabajo que su enemigo le deseava tener para su vengança" (Covarr., p. 755). Pelagio is his own worst enemy, having fallen into his own snares.

75. These lines may be proverbial, according to the suggestion of Ricardo Arias ("Refranes y frases proverbiales en el teatro de Valdivielso", *Rev. de Archivos, Museos, y Bibliotecas*, 81 [1978], p. 288).

76. The reading of this line and the next is not easy. The Lanini copy has--for the first line--"que el orrible infierno espera", which is not much help.

77. *Fullero.* A card sharp, cheater at card games (Covarr., p. 615).

78. Both MSS read, "deseo traygo un vestido que darle", which is a syntactical monstrosity. I give what seems a sensible rearrangement of the line, although it is hypermetric by one syllable.

79. Line 1261-1262. The meaning seems to be that God, in choosing Mary as a bride, gave her a new life and--in that life--a new father. Ildefonso has not actually bestowed upon her "la vida del honor", but rather has restored it to her, exactly as Leocadia had earlier announced (11. 504-507).

80. *Alarbes.* A reduction of al-árabes and, by extension, it means rude, barbarous, and bestial. See *Dicc. Aut.*, I, 158.

81. I have not been able to locate in Jeremiah the exact place in which these words are used.

82. *Christiano Adlante.* This was Atlas, King of Mauritania, who, because of his vast knowledge of the sun, moon, and stars, was said to have held the world on his shoulders. That Ilde-

fonso is called by Mary a Christian Atlas, supporting the
cause of devotion to her purity, is a signal acknowledge-
ment from Heaven of the worth it places on such steadfast-
ness.

83. At line 1289 there occurs the sole case of the use of diaere-
sis ("süaves") in the *Descensión* for metrical purposes.

84. The masculine article of the MS is preserved.

85. The Roxas copy reads "constantes"; the Lanini copy employs
the singular, "constante". I have left it in the plural, re-
specting Roxas' text, even though the agreement with "llamas" seems less apt than the singular agreement with "çarça"
(the bush it was that was constant, untouched by the flames).
The reference can be found in Exodus 3:2.

86. The unexpected brilliance forces Ildefonso to seek a suita-
ble comparison, and he finds it in the light with which
Elias is carried up to Heaven (IV Kings 2:1-18, at v. 11).
Elias, furthermore, was--like Ildefonso--a lifelong virgin.
See, for example, Saint Ambrose, *De virginibus* I, 3, 12.

87. In the Apocalypse of Saint John 4:6-7, God is seen seated,
surrounded by the twelve Patriarchs and the twelve Apostles,
attended also by figures representing the Evangelists:
Matthew as half-man, half animal; Mark as a lion; Luke as a
bullock; and John as an eagle. Valdivielso had already al-
luded to Ildefonso as a second John (ll. 41-44) and here con-
tinues the association, although with novel variations: as
John saw Heaven with God and the animals, so Ildefonso sees
it with Mary and "sin los animales" and "no lleno de Dios".

88. Lines 1316-1319. Saint Stephen, having defended his accurate knowledge of the events and personages of Biblical history before his enemies at a trumped-up trial, was permitted
a vision of Heaven, his face bathed in a strange light: "Ecce
video caelos apertos, et Filium hominis stantem a dextris
Dei" (Acts VI:55). Then he was taken out and stoned. The
difference is that Ildefonso is permitted to see Mary, not
God and His Son (who sent her). Valdivielso had used this
same sequence and comparison in *Sagrario de Toledo*, Bk. XVII,
301v.

89. Almost all of the *octavas* from this point on appear, with minor
variants, in *Sagrario de Toledo*. It seems that the originals
were those of the epic poem; Valdivielso borrowed them for the
auto. This stanza appears in the longer work in Book XVII, 302v

90. For Elvidiano, see also note 55 (for l. 783), where the form
was shortened ("Elvidio") for metrical reasons. In *Sagrario*
the line reads: "y vivirá, a pesar del tiempo cano"; as we
see, Valdivieso was forced on occasion to modify his text for
use in the new *auto*.

91. A proverbial phrase. "Al buen pagador, no le duelen prendas" (Correas, 42a).

92. This *octava* is *Sagrario*, Book XVII, 302v.

93. Atropos and Clotho are two of the trio (Lachesis is the third) of Fates. The first-named spun the thread, Lachesis wound it, and Clotho snipped it.

94. This stanza follows the preceding one (in *Sagrario*) after seven others have unfolded, and appears in Book XVII at 304r with one notable change, concerning line 1360. What had been "Mendoça valeroso" is changed to "Ylefonso valeroso". Elsewhere in the *auto* (1. 521), Ildefonso is called "Mendoça generoso".

95. Lines 1375-1378. At l. 1377 Roxas' copy has; "si vino con el Sol en tus entrañas", which makes no sense. I have retouched the line from the appropriate stanza in *Sagrario* (Book XVII, 306r), from which I give her the four relevant lines:

> ¿De dónde a mí que en cuerpo y alma venga
> La hermosa madre del Señor que adoro,
> Si bien no con el Sol en las entrañas,
> Mas hecha un Sol del Tajo a las montañas.

96. Lines 1380-1382. Three Angels of God appeared to Abraham and were given hospitality at his abode. Having dined, they told Abraham and Sarah that she would give birth. Ildefonso is amazed that he should be accorded similar, if not better, treatment by Heaven.

97. This stanza follows the preceding one also in *Sagrario* (Book XVII, 306r). The Biblical account is found in II Kings 6. Oza was struck down for touching the holy Ark of the Covenant while Obededon was much blessed for guarding it safely at home. Ildefonso feels even more blessed than Obededon for having preserved another Ark of God (Mary's virginal womb) from danger (the Pelagian heresy).

98. Cf. *Sagrario*, Book XVII, 307v.

99. Cf. *Sagrario*, Book XVII, 309v.

100. From Psalm 103: 18: "Montes excelsi cervis: petra refugium herinaciis". The image intensifies the notion of safe refuge which, for the future faithful, the stone on which the Virgin's foot has made an imprint will represent.

101. Cf. *Sagrario*, Book XVII, 310r.

102. This stanza is, basically, *Sagrario*, Book XVIII, 316v, but it has been extensively redesigned for the *auto*.

103. Cf. *Sagrario*, XVIII, 317v.

104. *Desalado*. With arms spread and seeking to follow, but unable to do so (des-alado). Roxas copy has "deshalado".

105. Lines 1434-1435 are difficult lines and I understand them as follows: "Even though my vestment ("palio") is given to me by Mary ("mejor Elías"), I will continue to honor ("voces daré") the humble, everyday ones (with which Ildefonso performs his ecclesiastical duties in Toledo)." This reading would be in perfect consonance with most earlier accounts of Ildefonso'e behavior after the visit: he returns to his customary routines and serves Mary even more until he is called to Heaven. One problem is the antecedent for the plural "mías".

106. This stanza and the one that follows occur in sequence also in *Sagrario*, Book XIX, 346r, with only slight variations.

107. The stanza duplicates *Sagrario*, Book XIX, 349v. The "voz de Faraón" is, of course, Moses. Ildefonso, preparing to return to the throng awaiting him outside the cathedral, is compared to Moses (returning with the Laws) when he prepares to meet the anxious and expectant Hebrews gathered at the foot of Mount Sion. See Exodus, chapter 24.

108. The first three lines of this final *octava* are, with one minor variation, the same as *Sagrario*, Book XIX, 349v (following the preceding stanza). Valdivielso introduces significant changes in the concluding five lines in order to end the text of the *Descensión*. For the sake of contrast, here are the *Sagrario* verses:

> A Ilefonso esperaban sus criados:
> Quando con rayos de hermosura llenos
> De la madre del Sol comunicados,
> Sale del alma Virgen la privança,
> Que todo quanto quiere della alcança.

63

BIBLIOGRAPHY

AGUIRRE, J. M., *José de Valdivielso y la poesía religiosa tradicional* (Toledo: I. P. I. E. T., 1965).

ALLUE Y MORER, F., "Centenario de un poeta: el Mro. Joseph de Valdivielso", *Poesía española*, Second Series, no. 90 (Junio 1960), 22-29.

ARIAS, Ricardo, "Refranes y frases proverbiales en el teatro de Valdivielso", *Revista de Archivos, Museos y Bibliotecas*, 81 (1978), 241-288.

---, *The Spanish Sacramental Plays* (Boston: Twayne, 1980), 111-121.

BRAEGELMAN, A., *The Life and Writings of Saint Ildefonsus of Toledo* (Washington, D. C.: The Catholic Univ. Press, 1942).

CANAL, J. M., "San Hildefonso de Toledo, historia y leyenda", *Ephemerides Mariologicae*, 17 (1967), 437-462.

CUSTODIO VEGA, Angel, "De patrología española: San Ildefonso de Toledo, sus biografías y sus biógrafos", *Boletín de la Real Academia de la Historia*, 145 (1969), 35-107.

DEVOTO, Daniel, "Tres notas sobre Berceo y la historia eclesiástica. I: Alba o casulla; ofrenda", *Bulletin Hispanique*, 70 (1968), 261-287.

ENTRAMBASAGUAS, Joaquín de, *Lope de Vega en las Justas Poéticas toledanas de 1605 y 1608* (Madrid, 1969).

---, *Lope de Vega y su tiempo*, I (Barcelona: Teide, 1961).

---, "Una nota lopiana y otra gongorina en una comedia del Fénix", *Revista de filología española*, 55 (1972), 309-314.

FERNANDEZ-PRIETO DOMINGUEZ, Enrique, *Actas de visitas reales . . . a los cuerpos de San Ildefonso y San Atilano, años 1462-1960* (Zamora: Tip. "Heraldo de Zamora", 1973).

HERRERA, Pedro de, *Descripción de la Capilla de Nuestra Señora del Sagrario* (Madrid: Luis Sánchez, 1617).

LA BARRERA Y LEIRADO, Cayetano A. de, *Catálogo bibliográfico y biográfico del teatro español antiguo desde sus orígenes hasta mediados del siglo XVIII* (Madrid, 1860; rpt. Madrid: Gredos, 1969).

MADOZ, José, "San Ildefonso de Toledo", *Estudios eclesiásticos*, 26 (1952), 467-505.

MARAÑON, Gregorio, *El Greco y Toledo* (Madrid: Espasa-Calpe, 1956).

MARTINEZ ARANCON, Ana, *La batalla en torno a Góngora* (Barcelona: A. Bosch, 1978).

MILLE Y GIMENEZ, Juan, "El papel de la nueva poesía (Lope, Góngora y los orígenes del culteranismo)", in *Estudios de literatura española* (La Plata: Fac. de Letras y Ciencias de Educación, 1928), 181-228.

MORLEY, S. G., and C. BRUERTON, *Cronología de las comedias de Lope de Vega* (Madrid: Gredos, 1968), 296-298.

PEREZ PASTOR, C., *Bibliografía madrileña de los siglos XVI-XVII. 2. 1601-1620* (Madrid, 1906; rpt. Amsterdam: Van Heusden, 1971).

PORTOCARRERO, Francisco, *Libro de la descensión de Nuestra Señora a la Santa Iglesia de Toledo, y vida de San Ildefonso, arzobispo della* (Madrid: Luis Sánchez, 1616).

RIVERA-RECIO, J., "Los Arzobispos de Toledo", *Anales toledanos*, 3 (1971), 193-203.

ROUANET, Léo, "Un auto inédit de Valdivielso", *Homenaje a Menéndez y Pelayo*, I (Madrid, 1899), 57-62.

SAINZ DE ROBLES, F. C., *Lope de Vega* (Madrid: Espasa-Calpe, 1962).

SIMON DIAZ, José, "Textos dispersos de clásicos españoles, XI: Valdivielso", *Revista de literatura*, 19 (1961), 125-168; 20 (1960), 407-436.

TAMAYO Y VARGAS, Tomás, *Defensa de la Descensión de la Virgen Nuestra Señora . . . a dar la casulla a su B. Capellán San Ilefonso* (Toledo: Diego Rodríguez, 1616).

VALDIVIELSO, José de, *Sagrario de Toledo* (Toledo: Luis Sánchez, 1616).

TABLE OF CONTENTS